Uncertain Reasoning in Justification Logic

Inauguraldissertation
der Philosophisch-naturwissenschaftlichen Fakultät
der Universität Bern

vorgelegt von
Ioannis Kokkinis
aus Griechenland

Leiter der Arbeit:
Prof. Dr. Thomas Studer
Institut für Informatik

Von der Philosophisch-naturwissenschaftlichen Fakultät angenommen.

Bern, den 20. Juni 2016   Der Dekan:
Prof. Dr. Gilberto Colangelo

Abstract

This thesis studies the combination of two well known formal systems for knowledge representation: probabilistic logic and justification logic. Our aim is to design a formal framework that allows the analysis of epistemic situations with incomplete information. In order to achieve this we introduce two probabilistic justification logics, which are defined by adding probability operators to the minimal justification logic J. We prove soundness and completeness theorems for our logics and establish decidability procedures. Both our logics rely on an infinitary rule so that strong completeness can be achieved. One of the most interesting mathematical results for our logics is the fact that adding only one iteration of the probability operator to the justification logic J does not increase the computational complexity of the logic.

Acknowledgements

First and foremost, I am deeply grateful to Thomas Studer. He has been an excellent supervisor and at the same time co-author. This thesis is mainly based on his ideas and without his guidance and support, it would have been impossible for me to successfully finish it. I am also thankful to Gerhard Jäger, since he has been an excellent teacher and employer. This thesis is also based on many ideas from Zoran Ognjanović. The interesting discussions I had with him in Dubrovnik helped me to clarify many issues. I am very thankful to him for his support. I would like to thank Nebojša Ikodinović for carefully reading this thesis and for providing useful comments that improved the quality of this work substantially.

I want to thank Stathis Zachos and Roman Kuznets for helping me start my PhD at the University of Bern. Stathis Zachos is also responsible for making me follow this area of research. By listening to his talks as an undergraduate student, I was convinced that theoretical computer science is a very interesting topic. I also want to thank the members of the Logic and Theory Group for the four wonderful years I spent working with them.

Last but not least, I want to thank my father, my mother and my older sister. Without their love and support, it would have been impossible for me to successfully complete my studies. This thesis is dedicated to them.

Contents

Abstract   iii

Acknowledgements   v

Contents   vii

1 Introduction   **1**
    1.1 Justification Logic 1
    1.2 Probabilistic Logic 2
    1.3 Probabilistic Justification Logic 3
    1.4 Related Work 5
    1.5 Overview of the Thesis 6

2 The Justification Logic J   **9**
    2.1 Syntax 9
    2.2 Semantics 12
    2.3 Fundamental Properties 14

3 Probabilistic Justification Logics   **17**
    3.1 The Probabilistic Justification Logic PJ 17
    3.2 Properties of the Logic PJ 24
    3.3 The Probabilistic Justification Logic PPJ 30
    3.4 Application to the Lottery Paradox 34

4 Soundness and Completeness — 37
- 4.1 Soundness — 37
- 4.2 Strong Completeness for PJ — 41
- 4.3 Strong Completeness for PPJ — 54

5 Decidability and Complexity — 63
- 5.1 Small Model Property for PJ — 63
- 5.2 Complexity Bounds for PJ — 73
- 5.3 Decidability for PPJ — 76

6 Conclusion and Further Work — 89

Bibliography — 93

Index — 99

Chapter 1

Introduction

In Sections 1.1 and 1.2 we give a short introduction to justification logics and probabilistic logics. In Section 1.3 we give an example of a problem which can be modelled neither in the language of justification logic nor in the language of probabilistic logic. This explains why a framework for uncertain reasoning in justification logic should be developed. In Section 1.3 we also give a small introduction to our framework for probabilistic justification logic. In Section 1.4 we compare our approach for modelling uncertain reasoning in justification logic with other approaches that were developed at approximately the same time with ours. We close this chapter by giving a short summary of the thesis in Section 1.5.

1.1 Justification Logic

The description of knowledge as "justified true belief" is usually attributed to Plato. While traditional modal epistemic logic [BdRV01] uses formulas of the form $\Box \alpha$ to express that an agent believes/knows α, the language of justification logic [AF15, Stu12] 'unfolds' the $\Box$-modality into a family of so-called *justification terms*, which are used to represent evidence for the agent's belief/knowledge. Hence, instead of $\Box \alpha$, justification logic includes formulas of the form $t : \alpha$ meaning

the agent believes α for reason t.

Artemov developed the first justification logic, the Logic of Proofs (usually abbreviated to LP), to provide intuitionistic logic with a classical provability semantics [Art95, Art01, KSar]. There, justification evidence terms represent formal proofs in Peano Arithmetic. However, justification terms can be used to represent evidence of more informal nature. This more general reading of terms lead to the development of justification logics for various purposes and applications [BKS11a, BKS11b, KS13, KS12, BKS14].

Melvin Fitting [Fit05] introduced the use of Kripke models in justification logic. However, semantics to justification logics can also be given by the so-called basic modular models. Artemov [Art12] initially proposed these models to provide an ontologically transparent semantics for justifications. Kuznets and Studer [KS12] further developed basic modular models so that they can provide semantics to many different justification logics. Note that basic modular models are mathematically equivalent to appropriate adaptations of Mkrtychev models [Mkr97] which were introduced earlier.

It is interesting that a famous correspondence between modal logics and justification logics has been established. Artemov [Art01] proved that any theorem in **LP** can be translated into a theorem in modal logic **S4** by replacing any justification term by the modal operator $\Box$ and that any theorem in **S4** can be translated into a theorem in **LP** by replacing any occurrence of a $\Box$ by an appropriate justification term. So, we say that **LP** realizes **S4**, or that **LP** is the explicit counterpart of **S4**. In the same way explicit counterparts for many famous modal logics were found [Bre00]. For example, the minimal modal logic **K** corresponds to basic the justification logic **J**.

1.2 Probabilistic Logic

The idea of probabilistic logics was first proposed by Leibnitz and subsequently discussed by a number of his successors, such as Jacobus Bernoulli, Lambert, Boole, etc. The modern development of this topic, however, started only in the late 1970s and was initiated by H. Jerome Keisler in his seminal paper [Kei77], where he introduced probability quantifiers of the form $Px > r$ (meaning that the probability of a set of objects is greater than r), thus providing a model-theoretic approach to the field. Another important effort came from Nils Nilsson, who tried to provide a logical framework for uncertain reasoning in [Nil86]. For example, he was able to formulate a probabilistic generalization of *modus ponens* as:

if α holds with probability s and β follows from α with probability t, then the probability of β is r.

Following Nilsson, a number of logical systems appeared (see [ORM09] for references) that extended the classical language with different probability operators. The standard semantics for this kind of probability logic is a special kind of Kripke models, where the accessibility relation between worlds is replaced with a finitely additive probability measure. As usual, the main logical problems in the proof-theoretical framework concern providing a sound and complete axiomatic system and decidability.

In fact, there are two kinds of completeness theorems: the simple completeness (every consistent formula is satisfiable) and the strong completeness theorem (every consistent set of formulas is satisfiable). In the first paper [FHM90] along the lines of Nilsson's research, Fagin, Halpern and Meggido introduced a logic with arithmetical operations built into the syntax so that Boolean combinations of linear inequalities of probabilities of formulas can be expressed. A finite axiomatic system is given and proved to be simply complete. However, the corresponding strong completeness does not follow immediately (as in classical logic) because of the lack of compactness: there are unsatisfiable sets of formulas that are finitely satisfiable. An example is the set of probabilistic constraints saying that the probability of a formula is not zero, but that it is less than any positive rational number. Concerning this issue, the main contribution of [OR99, RO99, OR00, SO14] was the introduction of several infinitary inference rules (rules with countably many premises and one conclusion) that allowed proofs of strong completeness in the corresponding logics. On the other hand, already in Boole's "Laws of Thought" a procedure of reducing sets of probabilistic constraints to systems of linear (in)equalities was provided. The same idea was used to prove decidability for most of propositional logics with probabilistic operators. Moreover, it was shown in [FHM90] that the satisfiability problem for the logic with linear combinations of probabilities is NP-complete, that is no worse than the corresponding problem in classical propositional logic.

1.3 Probabilistic Justification Logic

In Sections 1.1 and 1.2 we described two famous systems that can be used for reasoning about knowledge (justification logic) and uncertainty (probabilistic logic). In everyday life we often have to deal with incomplete evidence which naturally lead to vague justifications. So, it seems necessary to combine reasoning about knowledge and uncertainty. Let us consider the following example.

> **Motivating Example**
> Peter receives a phone call from Marc. Marc tells Peter that tax rates will increase. Peter reads in the New York Times that tax rates will increase. Peter considers the New York Times to be a much more reliable source than Marc.

In order to describe the situation in the Motivating Example, Peter needs a framework that allows reasoning about justifications and uncertainty together. Peter for example needs to say that "The probability of the fact that tax rates will increase, because Marc said so, is 30%" or that "The probability of the fact that tax rates will increase, because it is written in the New York times, is 80%". The languages of justification logic and probabilistic logic does not suffice for expressing such statements. However these kind of statements can be nicely expressed in probabilistic justification logic, which is a framework that allows reasoning about the probabilities of justified statements.

In this thesis we describe the probabilistic justification logic PJ [KMOS15], which is a combination of justification logic and probabilistic logic that makes it possible to adequately model different degrees of justification. The design of PJ follows that of LPP_2 [ORM09], which is a probablistic logic over classical propositional logic. The new operators that PJ introduces are the probability operators $P_{\geq s}$ where s is a rational number between 0 and 1. So, in the language of PJ statements of the form "$P_{\geq s}\alpha$" can be expressed, meaning that

the probability of truthfulness of the justification formula α is at least s.

Hence we can study, for instance, the formula

$$P_{\geq r}(u : (\alpha \to \beta)) \to \left(P_{\geq s}(v : \alpha) \to P_{\geq r \cdot s}(u \cdot v : \beta)\right), \tag{1.1}$$

which states that the probability of the conclusion of an application axiom is greater than or equal to the product of the probabilities of its premises. We will see later that this, of course, only holds in models where the premises are independent.

The semantics of PJ consists of a set of possible worlds, each a model of justification logic, and a probability measure $\mu(\cdot)$ on sets of possible worlds. We assign a probability to a formula α of justification logic as follows. We first determine the set $[\alpha]$ of possible worlds that satisfy α. Then we obtain the probability of α as $\mu([\alpha])$, i.e. by applying the measure function to the set $[\alpha]$. Hence our logic relies on the usual model of probability. This makes it possible, e.g., to explore the role of independence and to investigate formulas like (1.1) in full generality.

As it was mentioned in Section 1.2 there is an unpleasant consequence of a finitary axiomatization (i.e. an axiomatization where the proofs are always finite) in a language like the one of PJ: there exist consistent sets that are not satisfiable. This results from the inherent non-compactness of such systems. Consider for example the set $X = \left\{\neg P_{=0}\alpha\right\} \cup \left\{P_{<1/n}\alpha \mid n \in \mathbb{N}\right\}$. Although it is obvious that X cannot be satisfied, in a finitaty axiomatization it would be consistent: it is impossible to derive falsity from X since every proof from X would contain only a finite number of X elements. However, if proofs are allowed to be infinite, we can define an axiomatization in which X would not be consistent. Hence, in order to achieve strong completeness, our axiomatization of PJ should have an infinitary rule, i.e. a rule which has countably infinite premises and one conclusion.

The logic PJ does neither support iterations of the probability operators nor justification operators over probability operators. In this thesis we also present the logic PPJ [KOS16] that remedies these shortcomings. The axiomatization, semantics, soundness, completeness and decidability procedures for PPJ are obtained by combining results from the probabilistic logic LPP_1 [ORM09] and the justification logic J [AF15]. Note that these combinations are highly non-trivial due to the presence of formulas of the form $t : P_{\geq s}A$. Moreover, using PPJ we are able to provide a formal analysis of Kyburg's famous lottery paradox [Kyb61]. Probabilistic justification logics are intended for comparing different sources of information. Thus the key idea behind the introduction of logics PJ and PPJ is that:

$$\text{different kinds of evidence for } \alpha \\ \text{lead to different degrees of belief in } \alpha. \qquad (1.2)$$

1.4 Related Work

So far, probabilistic justification logics have not been investigated. Closely related are Milnikel's proposal [Mil14] for a system with uncertain justifications, Ghari's preprint [Gha14] introducing fuzzy justification logics and the possibilistic justification logic, which is an explicit version of a graded modal logic and was introduced by Fan and Liau in [FL15].

Milnikel introduces formulas of the form $t :_q \alpha$, which correspond to our $P_{\geq q}(t : \alpha)$. However, there are two important differences with our current work.

First, his semantics is completely different from the one we study. Instead of using a probability space, Milnikel uses a variation of Kripke-Fitting models. In his models, each triple (w, t, α) (of world, term and formula) is assigned an interval $E(w, t, \alpha)$ of the form $[0, r)$ or $[0, r]$ where r is a rational number from $[0, 1]$. Then the formula $t :_q \alpha$ is true at a world w iff $q \in E(w, t, \alpha)$ and also α is true in all worlds accessible from w. Because of this interval semantics, Milnikel can dispense with infinitary rules.

Second, Milnikel implicitly assumes that various pieces of evidence are independent. Hence the formula corresponding to (1.1) is an axiom in his system whereas

(1.1) may or may not hold in a model of our probabilistic justification logics depending on the independence of the premises of (1.1) in the given model.

Ghari presents various justification logics where he replaces the classical base with well-known fuzzy logics. In particular, he studies a justification logic **RPLJ** that is defined over Pavelka logic, which includes constants for all rational numbers in the interval $[0,1]$. This allows him to express statements of the form t *is a justification for believing α with certainty degree at least r*. Ghari shows that all principles of Milnikel's logic of uncertain justifications are valid in **RPLJ**.

The logic of Fan and Liau includes formulas $t :_r A$ to express that *according to evidence t, A is believed with certainty at least r*. However, the following principle holds in their logic:
$$s :_r A \wedge t :_q A \to s :_{\max(r,q)} A.$$

Hence all justifications for a belief yield the same (strongest) certainty, which is not in accordance with our guiding idea (1.2).

The combination of evidenced-based reasoning and reasoning under uncertainty has also been studied by Artemov in [Art16] and Schechter in [Sch15]. Schechter combined features from justification logics and logics of plausibility based beliefs to build a normal modal logic of explicit beliefs, where each agent can explicitly state which is their justification for believing in a given sentence. Artemov studied a justification logic to formalize aggregated probabilistic evidence. His approach can handle conflicting and inconsistent data and positive and negative evidence for the same proposition as well.

1.5 Overview of the Thesis

The chapters of the thesis are organized as follows:

In Chapter 2 we recall the the minimal justification logic J. We present the syntax, semantics and some fundamental results about the logic J.

In Chapter 3 we present the syntax and semantics for the probabilistic justification logics PJ and PPJ. We also illustrate the expressive power of probabilistic justification logic by formalizing Kyburg's lottery paradox in the language of PPJ.

In Chapter 4 we prove soundness and completeness results for the logics PJ and PPJ. Since PJ and PPJ make use of an infinitary rule we have to employ the Archimedean property for the real numbers in order to prove soundness. Completeness is proved by a canonical model construction.

In Chapter 5 we present decidability and complexity results for the satisfiability

1.5. OVERVIEW OF THE THESIS

problem in the logics PJ and PPJ. For both logics we reduce the satisfiability problem to solving a finite system of linear equations, which implies that the satisfiability problem is decidable. In the case of PJ we also establish some complexity bounds.

We close the thesis with some discussion and ideas for further work in Chapter 6.

This thesis is entirely based on results from [Kok16, KOS16, KMOS15].

Chapter 2

The Justification Logic J

In this section we present the basic justification logic J. We introduce its syntax and semantics and recall some fundamental properties of J.

2.1 Syntax

The language of justification logic is obtained by extending the language of classical propositional logic with formulas of the form $t : \alpha$, which are called *justification assertions*. In the formula $t : \alpha$, t is a justification term, which is usually used to represent evidence, and α is a justification formula, which is usually used to represent statements or facts. $t : \alpha$ reads as t *is a justification for believing* α.

Justification terms are built from countably many constants and countably many variables according to the following grammar:

$$t ::= c \mid x \mid (t \cdot t) \mid (t + t) \mid {!t}$$

where c is a constant and x is a variable. Tm denotes the set of all terms and Con denotes the set of all constants. For any term t and any non-negative integer n we define:

$$!^0 t := t \quad \text{and} \quad !^{n+1} t := !\,(!^n t) \ .$$

We assume that ! has greater precedence than $\cdot$, which has greater precedence than $+$. The operators $\cdot$ and $+$ are assumed to be left-associative.

As already mentioned terms are used to provide justifications (or proofs) for formulas. Term constants are used as justifications for axioms, whereas term variables are used as justifications for arbitrary formulas. The operator $\cdot$ can be used by the agent to apply modus ponens (see axiom (J) in Figure 2.1.1), the operator $+$

is used for concatenating proofs (see axiom (+) in Figure 2.1.1) and the operator ! is used for verifying evidence (see rule (AN!) in Figure 2.1.2). That is, if the agent has a justification c for α then he has a justification $!c$ for the fact that c is a justification for α and so on.

Let Prop denote a countable set of atomic propositions. Formulas of the language $\mathcal{L}_J$ (justification formulas) are built according to the following grammar:

$$\alpha ::= p \mid \neg \alpha \mid \alpha \wedge \alpha \mid t : \alpha$$

where $t \in \mathsf{Tm}$ and $p \in \mathsf{Prop}$. In the sequel we will use the Greek letters $\alpha, \beta, \gamma, \ldots$ for elements of $\mathcal{L}_J$ and the letter p for elements of Prop all of them possibly primed or with subscripts. We will also use the symbol $\mathbb{N}$ to represent the set of all natural numbers.

We define the following abbreviations in the standard way:

$$\alpha \vee \beta \equiv \neg(\neg \alpha \wedge \neg \beta) \ ;$$
$$\alpha \to \beta \equiv \neg \alpha \vee \beta \ ;$$
$$\alpha \leftrightarrow \beta \equiv (\alpha \to \beta) \wedge (\beta \to \alpha) \ ;$$
$$\bot \equiv \alpha \wedge \neg \alpha, \text{ for some } \alpha \in \mathcal{L}_J \ ;$$
$$\top \equiv \alpha \vee \neg \alpha, \text{ for some } \alpha \in \mathcal{L}_J \ .$$

We assume that : and $\neg$ have higher precedence than $\wedge$ and $\vee$, which have higher precedence than $\to$ and $\leftrightarrow$. Sometimes we will write $\alpha_1, \ldots, \alpha_n$ instead of $\{\alpha_1\} \cup \cdots \cup \{\alpha_n\}$ as well as T, α instead of $T \cup \{\alpha\}$ and X, Y instead of $X \cup Y$.

Definition 2.1.1 (Logic). A logic over some language $\mathcal{L}$ is a formal system that consists of a set of axiom schemata and inference rules together with a provability relation and a satisfiability relation. We will use the symbols L, $\vdash$ and $\models$ to describe a logic, a provability relation and a satisfiability relation respectively. All the logics we are going to consider will be extensions of classical propositional logic.

In Figure 2.1.1 we present the axiom schemata for the logic J. Axiom (J) is also called the application axiom and is the justification logic analogue of the rule modus ponens. It states that we can combine a justification for $\alpha \to \beta$ and a justification for α to obtain a justification for β. Axiom (+), which is also called the monotonicity axiom, states that if u or v is a justification for α then the term $u + v$ is also a justification for α.

2.1. SYNTAX

> (P) finite set of axioms schemata axiomatizing classical propositional logic in the language of $\mathcal{L}_J$
> (J) $\vdash u : (\alpha \to \beta) \to (v : \alpha \to u \cdot v : \beta)$
> (+) $\vdash (u : \alpha \lor v : \alpha) \to u + v : \alpha$

Figure 2.1.1: Axioms Schemata for the Logic J

Let L be a logic. A *constant specification* for the logic L is any set CS that satisfies the following condition:

$$CS \subseteq \{(c, \alpha) \mid c \in Con \text{ and } \alpha \text{ is an instance of some L-axiom scheme}\}.$$

As we will see later the constant specification determines some axiom instances for which the logic provides justifications (without any proof).

A constant specification CS for a logic L will be called:

axiomatically appropriate: if for every instance of an L-axiom scheme, α, there exists some constant c such that $(c, \alpha) \in$ CS, i.e. if every axiom of L is justified by at least one constant.

schematic: if for every constant c the set

$$\{\alpha \mid (c, \alpha) \in CS\}$$

consists of all instances of several (possibly zero) axiom schemata, i.e. every constant specifies certain axiom schemata and only them.

decidable: if the set CS is decidable. In the sequel when we refer to a decidable CS, we will always imply that CS is decidable in *polynomial time*.

finite: if CS is a finite set.

total: if for every term constant c and every axiom of L, $(c, \alpha) \in$ CS.

Let CS be any constant specification for the logic J. The deductive system J_{CS} is the Hilbert system obtained by adding to the axioms of J the rules modus ponens, (MP), and axiom necessitation, (AN!), as one can see in Figure 2.1.2. Rule (AN!) makes the connection between the constant specification and the proofs in J_{CS}: if $(c, \alpha) \in$ CS then we can prove that c is justification for α, that $!c$ is a justification for $c : \alpha$ and so on.

> axiom schemata of J
> +
> (MP) if $T \vdash \alpha$ and $T \vdash \alpha \to \beta$ then $T \vdash \beta$
> (AN!) $\vdash !^n c : !^{n-1} c : \cdots : !c : c : \alpha$, where $(c, \alpha) \in \mathsf{CS}$ and $n \in \mathbb{N}$

Figure 2.1.2: System $\mathsf{J_{CS}}$

Let L be a logic. As usual $T \vdash_\mathsf{L} \alpha$ means that the formula α is deducible (or derivable) from the set of formulas T using the rules and axioms of L. When L is clear from the context, it will be omitted. A formula α is a theorem ($\vdash A$) if it is deducible from the empty set.

Let L be a logic over the language $\mathcal{L}$. A set T is said to be L-*deductively closed* for $\mathcal{L}$ iff for every $\alpha \in \mathcal{L}$:

$$T \vdash_\mathsf{L} \alpha \iff \alpha \in T.$$

2.2 Semantics

The models for the logic J which we are going to present in this section were introduced by Mkrtychev [Mkr97] for the logic LP. Later Kuznets [Kuz00] adapted these models for other justification logics (including J) and proved the corresponding soundness and completeness theorems. The key notion about this semantics is the notion of a CS-evaluation. We use T to represent the truth value "true" and F to represent the truth value "false". Let $\mathcal{P}(W)$ denote the powerset of the set W.

Definition 2.2.1 (CS-Evaluation). Let L be a logic over some language $\mathcal{L}$. Let CS be any constant specification for L. A CS-evaluation, is a function $*$ that maps atomic propositions to truth values and maps justification terms to subsets of $\mathcal{L}$, i.e.:

$$* : \mathsf{Prop} \to \{\mathsf{T}, \mathsf{F}\} \text{ and}$$
$$* : \mathsf{Tm} \to \mathcal{P}(\mathcal{L}) ,$$

such that for $u, v \in \mathsf{Tm}$, for a constant c and $\alpha \in \mathcal{L}$ we have[1]:

(1) $\left(\alpha \to \beta \in u^* \text{ and } \alpha \in v^*\right) \implies \beta \in (u \cdot v)^*$;

(2) $u^* \cup v^* \subseteq (u + v)^*$;

---
[1] We will usually write t^* and p^* instead of $*(t)$ and $*(p)$ respectively.

2.2. SEMANTICS

(3) if $(c, \alpha) \in \mathsf{CS}$ then for all $n \in \mathbb{N}$ we have[2]:

$$!^{n-1}c : !^{n-2}c : \cdots :!c : c : \alpha \in (!^n c)^* \ .$$

So, a model for J_{CS}, or a J_{CS}-model, is a CS-evaluation.

Remark 2.2.2. As we already mentioned, the justification logic J is the minimal justification logic. Many justification logics can be defined by adding axioms to the logic J [AF15]. As we can see in Definition 2.2.1 the conditions that a CS-evaluation should satisfy, correspond only to the axioms of the logic J. Therefore, it might be more appropriate to use the name J_{CS}-evaluation instead of the name CS-evaluation. However, this thesis aims to provide a first study of the combination of probabilistic logic and justification logic. Therefore, we consider it useful to study the smallest possible framework. As a consequence, our logics will not contain any further justification axioms[3] than the ones from the basic logic J. Thus, for our purposes, the evaluation depends only on the constant specification CS.

Now we will define the binary relation $\models$.

Definition 2.2.3 (Truth under a CS-Evaluation). We define what it means for an $\mathcal{L}_\mathsf{J}$-formula to hold under a CS-evaluation $*$ inductively as follows:

$$* \models p \iff p^* = \mathsf{T} \quad \text{for } p \in \mathsf{Prop} \ ;$$
$$* \models \neg \alpha \iff * \not\models \alpha \ ;$$
$$* \models \alpha \wedge \beta \iff \bigl(* \models \alpha \text{ and } * \models \beta\bigr) \ ;$$
$$* \models t : \alpha \iff \alpha \in t^* \ .$$

Definition 2.2.4 (Satisfiability and Semantical Consequence in J). Let $T \subseteq \mathcal{L}_\mathsf{J}$, let $\alpha \in \mathcal{L}_\mathsf{J}$ and let $*$ be a CS-evaluation.

- We say that $*$ *satisfies* α iff $* \models \alpha$ holds.

- $* \models T$ means that $*$ *satisfies all the members* of the set T.

- We write $T \models_{\mathsf{CS}} \alpha$ (and read that α is a *semantical consequence* of T) to denote that for every CS-evaluation $*$, $* \models T$ implies $* \models \alpha$.

- α will be called J_{CS}-*satisfiable* or CS-*satisfiable* (or even simply satisfiable, if there is no danger of confusion) if there is a CS-evaluation that satisfies α.

---

[2] We agree to the convention that the formula $!^{n-1}c : !^{n-2}c : \cdots : !c : c : \alpha$ represents the formula α for $n = 0$.

[3] Of course our logics will contain probabilistic axioms as we will see later.

We close the section by defining two important decision problems that are related to the logic J.

Definition 2.2.5 (The J_{CS}-Satisfiability Problem). Let CS be any constant specification for the logic J. The J_{CS}-satisfiability problem or the satisfiability problem in the logic J_{CS} is the following decision problem:

for a given $\alpha \in \mathcal{L}_J$ is α CS-satisfiable?

Definition 2.2.6 (The J_{CS}-Derivability Problem). Let CS be any constant specification for the logic J. The J_{CS}-derivability problem or the derivability problem in the logic J_{CS} is the following decision problem:

for a given $\alpha \in \mathcal{L}_J$, is there a proof for α in J_{CS}?

2.3 Fundamental Properties

Internalization states that the logic internalizes the notion of its own proof, i.e. when we have a proof in a logic, then a formula that "encodes" this proof is provable in the logic. It is well known that internalization holds for the logic J. A proof of the following theorem can be found in [KS12].

Theorem 2.3.1 (Internalization). *Let CS be an axiomatically appropriate constant specification for the logic J. For any formulas $\alpha, \beta_1, \ldots, \beta_n \in \mathcal{L}_J$ and terms $t_1, \ldots, t_n$, if:*

$$\beta_1, \ldots, \beta_n \vdash_{J_{CS}} \alpha$$

then there exists a term t such that:

$$t_1 : \beta_1, \ldots, t_n : \beta_n \vdash_{J_{CS}} t : \alpha .$$

Observe that the version without premises is an explicit form of the necessitation rule of modal logic. Theorem 2.3.1 is sometimes called constructive necessitation.

The deduction theorem is standard for justification logic [Art01]. Therefore, we omit its proof here.

Theorem 2.3.2 (Deduction Theorem for J). *Let $T \subseteq \mathcal{L}_J$ and let $\alpha, \beta \in \mathcal{L}_J$. Then for any J_{CS} we have:*

$$T, \alpha \vdash_{J_{CS}} \beta \iff T \vdash_{J_{CS}} \alpha \to \beta .$$

Last but not least, we have soundness and completeness of J_{CS} with respect to CS-evaluations [Art12, KS12].

2.3. FUNDAMENTAL PROPERTIES

Theorem 2.3.3 (Soundness and Completeness of J). *Let* CS *be any constant specification for the logic* J. *Let* $\alpha \in \mathcal{L}_J$. *Then we have:*

$$\vdash_{J_{CS}} \alpha \quad \Longleftrightarrow \quad \models_{CS} \alpha .$$

We close this chapter by recalling the procedure that decides the satisfiability problem in the logic J_{CS}.

The first algorithm for the satisfiability problem in justification logics was presented by Artemov [Art95] for a finite constant specification in the logic LP. Later Mkrtychev [Mkr97] extended Artemov's result for a total constant specification. Mkrtychev's result was reproved and generalized for other justification logics (including J) by Kuznets [Kuz00]. Note that in [Kuz08] it is pointed out, that the satisfiability algorithm for the logic J from [Kuz00] also holds for a decidable and schematic constant specification.

Let CS be a decidable and schematic constant specification for the logic J. Kuznets' algorithm for the J_{CS}-satisfiability problem is divided in two parts: the *saturation algorithm* and the *completion algorithm*. Let $\alpha \in \mathcal{L}_J$ be the formula that is tested for satisfiability.

- The saturation algorithm produces a set of requirements that should be satisfied by any CS-evaluation that satisfies α. The saturation algorithm operates in NP-time[4].

- The completion algorithm determines whether a CS-evaluation that satisfies α exists or not. The completion algorithm operates in coNP-time.

If the saturation and the completion algorithm are taken together, then we obtain a Σ_2^p-algorithm for the J_{CS}-satisfiability problem.

The most crucial question in the completion algorithm is to decide whether a given term $t \in \text{Tm}$ justifies a formula $\alpha \in \mathcal{L}_J$. At a first point it might look that this problem is undecidable, since a given term may justify infinitely many formulas. For example some constant c from the constant specification may justify all the instances of an axiom scheme. This problem is solved by the fact that we restrict the constant specification to be schematic and by the fact that the logic J is axiomatized by finitely many axiom schemata. So, if we use schematic variables for formulas and terms we will have that every term justifies finitely

---

[4]A reader unfamiliar with notions of computational complexity theory may consult a textbook on the field, like [Pap94].

many (schematic) formulas. Of course, in order to answer the question whether a given term justifies some formula we need to find a set of formulas that belongs to two different schemata. This question is naturally answered by finding the most general unifier of the two schemata.

So, we have the following results.

Theorem 2.3.4. *Let* CS *be a decidable and schematic constant specification for the logic* J. *The* J_{CS}-*satisfiabilty problem belongs to the complexity class* Σ_2^p.

By a result from [Mil07] which was later strengthened in [BK12] and [Ach15] we have the following theorem:

Theorem 2.3.5. *Let* CS *be a decidable, schematic and axiomatically appropriate constant specification for the logic* J. *The* J_{CS}-*satisfiabilty problem belongs to the complexity class* Σ_2^p-*hard.*

By Theorems 2.3.4, 2.3.5 and 2.3.3 we get the following corollary:

Corollary 2.3.6. *Let* CS *be a decidable, schematic and axiomatically appropriate constant specification for the logic* J. *The* J_{CS}-*satisfiability problem is* Σ_2^p-*complete and the* J_{CS}-*derivability problem is* Π_2^p-*complete.*

Chapter 3

Probabilistic Justification Logics

In this chapter we present two probabilistic justification logics: the logic PJ that was introduced in [KMOS15] and the logic PPJ that was introduced in [KOS16]. We present syntax and semantics for these logics and also prove some properties for them. We also illustrate the expressive power of probabilistic justification logic by formalizing Kyburg's famous lottery pardox [Kyb61] in the logic PPJ.

3.1 The Probabilistic Justification Logic PJ

The probabilistic justification logic PJ is a probabilistic logic over the basic justification logic J. In this section we present the syntax and semantics for this logic.

Syntax

We will represent the set of all rational numbers with the symbol $\mathbb{Q}$. If X and Y are sets, we will sometimes write XY instead of $X \cap Y$. We define $\mathsf{S} := \mathbb{Q}[0,1]$. Thus, according to our notation $\mathsf{S}[0,t)$ denotes the set of all rational numbers greater than or equal to 0 and strictly less than t.

The formulas of the language $\mathcal{L}_{\mathsf{PJ}}$ (the so called probabilistic formulas) are built according to the following grammar:

$$A ::= P_{\geq s}\alpha \mid \neg A \mid A \wedge A$$

where $s \in \mathsf{S}$, and $\alpha \in \mathcal{L}_\mathsf{J}$. The intended meaning of the the formula $P_{\geq s}\alpha$ is that "the probability of truthfulness for the justification formula α" is at least s.

We assume the same abbreviations and the same precedence for the propositional connectives $\neg, \wedge, \vee, \rightarrow, \leftrightarrow$, as for the language $\mathcal{L}_\mathsf{J}$. However, we need to define a bottom and a top element for the language $\mathcal{L}_\mathsf{PJ}$. Hence, we define:

$$\bot := A \wedge \neg A, \text{ for some } A \in \mathcal{L}_\mathsf{PJ} ;$$
$$\top := A \vee \neg A, \text{ for some } A \in \mathcal{L}_\mathsf{PJ} .$$

It will always be clear from the context whether $\neg, \wedge, \top, \bot, \ldots$ refer to formulas of $\mathcal{L}_\mathsf{J}$ or $\mathcal{L}_\mathsf{PJ}$. The operator $P_{\geq s}$ is assumed to have greater precedence than all the propositional connectives. We will also use the following syntactical abbreviations:

$$P_{<s}\alpha \equiv \neg P_{\geq s}\alpha ;$$
$$P_{\leq s}\alpha \equiv P_{\geq 1-s}\neg\alpha ;$$
$$P_{>s}\alpha \equiv \neg P_{\leq s}\alpha ;$$
$$P_{=s}\alpha \equiv P_{\geq s}\alpha \wedge P_{\leq s}\alpha .$$

We will use capital Latin letters like A, B, C, ... for members of $\mathcal{L}_\mathsf{PJ}$ possibly primed or with subscripts.

The axiom schemata of the logic PJ are presented in Figure 3.1.1. Axiom (PI) corresponds to the fact that the probability of truthfulness of every justification formula is at least 0. Observe that by substituting $\neg\alpha$ for α in (PI), we have $P_{\geq 0}\neg\alpha$, which by our syntactical abbreviations is $P_{\leq 1}\alpha$. Hence axiom (PI) also corresponds to the fact that the probability of truthfulness of every justification formula is at most 1. Axioms (WE) and (LE) describe some properties of inequalities. Axioms (DIS) and (UN) correspond to the additivity of probabilities for disjoint events.

(P)		finitely many axiom schemata axiomatizing classical propositional logic in the language $\mathcal{L}_\mathsf{PJ}$
(PI)		$\vdash P_{\geq 0}\alpha$
(WE)		$\vdash P_{\leq r}\alpha \rightarrow P_{<s}\alpha$, where $s > r$
(LE)		$\vdash P_{<s}\alpha \rightarrow P_{\leq s}\alpha$
(DIS)		$\vdash P_{\geq r}\alpha \wedge P_{\geq s}\beta \wedge P_{\geq 1}\neg(\alpha \wedge \beta) \rightarrow P_{\geq \min(1,r+s)}(\alpha \vee \beta)$
(UN)		$\vdash P_{\leq r}\alpha \wedge P_{<s}\beta \rightarrow P_{<r+s}(\alpha \vee \beta)$, where $r + s \leq 1$

Figure 3.1.1: Axioms Schemata of PJ

It is very important to note the different uses of axiom (P). As an axiom of J, (P) contains all the propositional tautologies that are members of $\mathcal{L}_\mathsf{J}$, e.g. $t : \alpha \rightarrow t : \alpha$. As an axiom of PJ, (P) contains all the propositional tautologies that are members of $\mathcal{L}_\mathsf{PJ}$, e.g. $P_{\geq s}(t : \alpha) \rightarrow P_{\geq s}(t : \alpha)$.

3.1. THE PROBABILISTIC JUSTIFICATION LOGIC PJ

For any constant specification CS for the logic J the deductive system $\mathsf{PJ_{CS}}$ is the deductive system obtained by adding to the axiom schemata of PJ the rules (MP), (CE) and (ST) (see Figure 3.1.2). Rule (CE) makes the connection between justification logic and probabilistic logic possible. It states that if a justification formula is a validity, then it has probability 1. Rule (CE) can also be considered as the probabilistic analogue of the necessitation rule for modal logics. The rule (ST) intuitively states that if the probability of a justification formula is arbitrary close to s, then it is at least s. Observe that the rule (ST) is infinitary in the sense that it has an infinite number of premises. It corresponds to the Archimedean property for the real numbers (see Proposition 4.1.1).

A proof of an $\mathcal{L}_{\mathsf{PJ}}$-formula A from a set T of $\mathcal{L}_{\mathsf{PJ}}$-formulas is a sequence of formulas A_k indexed by countable ordinal numbers such that the last formula is A, and each formula in the sequence is an axiom, or a formula from T, or it is derived from the preceding formulas by a PJ-rule of inference.

axiom schemata of PJ
$+$
(MP)   if $T \vdash A$ and $T \vdash A \to B$ then $T \vdash B$
(CE)   if $\vdash_{\mathsf{J_{CS}}} \alpha$ then $\vdash_{\mathsf{PJ_{CS}}} P_{\geq 1}\alpha$
(ST)   if $T \vdash A \to P_{\geq s - \frac{1}{k}}\alpha$ for every integer $k \geq \frac{1}{s}$ and $s > 0$ then $T \vdash A \to P_{\geq s}\alpha$

Figure 3.1.2: System $\mathsf{PJ_{CS}}$

When we present proofs in a logic we are going to use the following abbreviations:

P.R.: it stands for "propositional reasoning". E.g. when we have $\vdash A \to B$ we can claim that by **P.R.** we get $\vdash \neg B \to \neg A$. We can think of **P.R.** as an abbreviation of the phrase "by some applications of (P) and (MP)".

S.E.: it stands for "syntactical equivalence". E.g. according to our syntactical conventions the formulas $P_{\geq 1-s}(\alpha \vee \beta)$ and $P_{\leq s}(\neg \alpha \wedge \neg \beta)$ are syntactically equivalent. We will transform our formulas to syntactically equivalent ones (using the syntactical abbreviations defined on Sections 2.1 and 3.1), in order to increase readability of our proofs. We have to be very careful when we apply **S.E.**. For example the formulas $P_{\geq s}(\neg \alpha \vee \beta)$ and $P_{\geq s}(\alpha \to \beta)$ are syntactically equivalent, whereas the formulas $P_{\geq s}\alpha$ and $P_{\geq s}\neg\neg\alpha$ are not.

i.h.: it stands for inductive hypothesis.

Semantics

A model for some PJ$_{CS}$ is a probability space. The universe of the probability space is a set of models for the logic J$_{CS}$ (i.e. a set of CS-evaluations). In order to determine the probability of a justification formula α in such a probability space we have to find the measure of the set containing all the CS-evaluations that satisfy α. The following definitions formalize the notions of a PJ$_{CS}$-model and the notion of satisfiability in a PJ$_{CS}$-model.

Definition 3.1.1 (Algebra Over a Set). Let W be a non-empty set and let H be a non-empty subset of $\mathcal{P}(W)$. H will be called an *algebra over* W iff the following hold:

- $W \in H$;
- $U, V \in H \implies U \cup V \in H$;
- $U \in H \implies W \setminus U \in H$.

Definition 3.1.2 (Finitely Additive Measure). Let H be an algebra over W and let $\mu : H \to [0,1]$. We call μ a *finitely additive measure* iff the following hold:

(1) $\mu(W) = 1$;

(2) for all $U, V \in H$:
$$U \cap V = \emptyset \implies \mu(U \cup V) = \mu(U) + \mu(V) .$$

Definition 3.1.3 (Probability Space). A *probability space* is a triple
$$\mathsf{Prob} = \langle W, H, \mu \rangle ,$$
where:

- W is a non-empty set ;
- H is an algebra over W ;
- $\mu : H \to [0,1]$ is a finitely additive measure.

The members of H are called measurable sets.

Definition 3.1.4 (PJ$_{CS}$-Model). Let CS be any constant specification for the logic J. A model for PJ$_{CS}$ or simply a PJ$_{CS}$-*model* is a structure $M = \langle W, H, \mu, * \rangle$ where:

- $\langle W, H, \mu \rangle$ is a probability space ;

3.1. THE PROBABILISTIC JUSTIFICATION LOGIC PJ

- $*$ is a function from W to the set of all CS-evaluations, i.e. $*(w)$ is a CS-evaluation for each world $w \in W$. We will usually write $*_w$ instead of $*(w)$.

The notion of independent setsin a model is defined as usual.

Definition 3.1.5 (Independent Sets in a $\mathsf{PJ_{CS}}$-Model). Let $M = \langle W, H, \mu, * \rangle$ be a model for some $\mathsf{PJ_{CS}}$ and let $U, V \in H$. U and V will be called *independent* in M iff the following holds:

$$\mu(U \cap V) = \mu(U) \cdot \mu(V) .$$

In order to determine the probability of a justification formula α, the set of worlds satisfying α should be measurable. Therefore we need the notion of a measurable model.

Definition 3.1.6 (Measurable Model). Let $M = \langle W, H, \mu, * \rangle$ be a model for some $\mathsf{PJ_{CS}}$ and let $\alpha \in \mathcal{L}_\mathsf{J}$. We define the following set:

$$[\alpha]_M = \{w \in W \mid *_w \models \alpha\} .$$

We will omit the subscript M, i.e. we will simply write $[\alpha]$, if M is clear from the context. A $\mathsf{PJ_{CS}}$-model $M = \langle W, H, \mu, * \rangle$ is *measurable* iff $[\alpha]_M \in H$ for every $\alpha \in \mathcal{L}_\mathsf{J}$. The class of measurable $\mathsf{PJ_{CS}}$-models will be denoted by $\mathsf{PJ_{CS,Meas}}$.

We have the following standard properties of a finitely additive measure.

Lemma 3.1.7 (Properties of a Finitely Additive Measure). *Let H be an algebra over some set W, let $\mu : H \to [0,1]$ be a finitely additive measure and let $U, V \in H$. Then the following hold:*

(1) $\mu(U \cup V) + \mu(U \cap V) = \mu(U) + \mu(V)$ *;*

(2) $\mu(U) + \mu(W \setminus U) = 1$ *;*

(3) $U \supseteq V \implies \mu(U) \geq \mu(V)$ *.*

Proof. Observe that since H is an algebra over W we have that $U \cup V$, $U \cap V$, $W \setminus U$, $U \setminus V$, and $V \setminus U$ belong to H.

(1) We have:

$$\mu(U \cup V) + \mu(U \cap V) =$$
$$\mu((U \setminus V) \cup (U \cap V) \cup (V \setminus U)) + \mu(U \cap V) .$$

And since the sets $(U \setminus V)$, $(U \cap V)$, $(V \setminus U)$ are mutually disjoint we get:

$$\mu(U \cup V) + \mu(U \cap V) =$$
$$\mu(U \setminus V) + \mu(U \cap V) + \mu(V \setminus U) + \mu(U \cap V) =$$
$$\mu((U \setminus V) \cup (U \cap V)) + \mu((V \setminus U) \cup (U \cap V)) =$$
$$\mu(U) + \mu(V) \ .$$

(2) It holds that:

$$1 = \mu(W) = \mu(U \cup (W \setminus U)) \stackrel{U \cap (W \setminus U) = \emptyset}{=} \mu(U) + \mu(W \setminus U) \ .$$

(3) Assume that $U \supseteq V$. We have that:

$$\mu(U) = \mu((U \setminus V) \cup V) \stackrel{V \cap (U \setminus V) = \emptyset}{=} \mu(U \setminus V) + \mu(V) \ .$$

And since $\mu(U \setminus V) \geq 0$ we get $\mu(U) \geq \mu(V)$. $\square$

Remark 3.1.8. Let $M = \langle W, H, \mu, * \rangle$ be a model for some $\mathsf{PJ_{CS}}$ and let $\alpha, \beta \in \mathcal{L}_\mathsf{J}$. It holds:

$$[\alpha \vee \beta]_M = \{w \in W \mid *_w \models \alpha \vee \beta\} = \{w \in W \mid *_w \models \alpha \text{ or } *_w \models \beta\} =$$
$$\{w \in W \mid *_w \models \alpha\} \cup \{w \in W \mid *_w \models \beta\} = [\alpha]_M \cup [\beta]_M \ ;$$
$$[\alpha \wedge \beta]_M = \{w \in W \mid *_w \models \alpha \wedge \beta\} = \{w \in W \mid *_w \models \alpha \text{ and } *_w \models \beta\} =$$
$$\{w \in W \mid *_w \models \alpha\} \cap \{w \in W \mid *_w \models \beta\} = [\alpha]_M \cap [\beta]_M \ ;$$
$$[\neg \alpha]_M = \{w \in W \mid *_w \models \neg \alpha\} = \{w \in W \mid *_w \not\models \alpha\} =$$
$$W \setminus \{w \in W \mid *_w \models \alpha\} = W \setminus [\alpha]_M \ .$$

Hence if $M \in \mathsf{PJ_{CS,Meas}}$ we get by Lemma 3.1.7:

$$\mu([\alpha \vee \beta]_M) + \mu([\alpha \wedge \beta]_M) = \mu([\alpha]_M) + \mu([\beta]_M) \ ;$$
$$\mu([\alpha]_M) + \mu([\neg \alpha]_M) = 1 \ .$$

Definition 3.1.9 (Truth in a $\mathsf{PJ_{CS,Meas}}$-model). Let CS be any constant specification for the logic J. Let $M = \langle W, H, \mu, * \rangle$ be a $\mathsf{PJ_{CS,Meas}}$-model. We define what it means for an $\mathcal{L}_\mathsf{PJ}$-formula to hold in M inductively as follows:

$$M \models P_{\geq s}\alpha \iff \mu([\alpha]_M) \geq s \ ;$$
$$M \models \neg A \iff M \not\models A \ ;$$
$$M \models A \wedge B \iff \left(M \models A \text{ and } M \models B\right) \ .$$

3.1. THE PROBABILISTIC JUSTIFICATION LOGIC PJ

Definition 3.1.10 (Satisfiability and Semantical Consequence in PJ). Assume that $T \subseteq \mathcal{L}_{\mathsf{PJ}}$, let $A \in \mathcal{L}_{\mathsf{PJ}}$ and let M be a $\mathsf{PJ}_{\mathsf{CS},\mathsf{Meas}}$-model.

- We say that M satisfies A iff $M \models A$ holds.
- $M \models T$ means that that M satisfies all the members of the set T.
- We write $T \models_{\mathsf{PJ}_{\mathsf{CS},\mathsf{Meas}}} A$ (and read that A is a semantical consequence of T) to denote that for every $\mathsf{PJ}_{\mathsf{CS},\mathsf{Meas}}$-model M, $M \models T$ implies $M \models A$.
- A will be called $\mathsf{PJ}_{\mathsf{CS},\mathsf{Meas}}$-satisfiable (or simply satisfiable, if there is no danger of confusion) if there is some $\mathsf{PJ}_{\mathsf{CS},\mathsf{Meas}}$-model M that satisfies A.

We now define two important decision problems that are related to the logic PJ.

Definition 3.1.11 (The $\mathsf{PJ}_{\mathsf{CS},\mathsf{Meas}}$-Satisfiability Problem). Let CS be any constant specification for the logic J. The $\mathsf{PJ}_{\mathsf{CS},\mathsf{Meas}}$-satisfiability problem or is the following decision problem:

$$\text{for a given } A \in \mathcal{L}_{\mathsf{PJ}} \text{ is } A \ \mathsf{PJ}_{\mathsf{CS},\mathsf{Meas}}\text{-satisfiable?}$$

Definition 3.1.12 (The $\mathsf{PJ}_{\mathsf{CS}}$-Derivability Problem). Let CS be any constant specification for the logic J. The $\mathsf{PJ}_{\mathsf{CS}}$-derivability problem or the derivability problem in the logic $\mathsf{PJ}_{\mathsf{CS}}$ is the following decision problem:

$$\text{for a given } A \in \mathcal{L}_{\mathsf{PJ}}, \text{ can we have a proof for } A \text{ in } \mathsf{PJ}_{\mathsf{CS}}?$$

Lemma 3.1.13 (Properties of the Class $\mathsf{PJ}_{\mathsf{CS},\mathsf{Meas}}$). *Let CS be any constant specification for the logic J, let $M = \langle W, H, \mu, * \rangle \in \mathsf{PJ}_{\mathsf{CS},\mathsf{Meas}}$ and let $\alpha \in \mathcal{L}_{\mathsf{J}}$. Then the following hold:*

(1) $M \models P_{\leq s}\alpha \iff \mu([\alpha]) \leq s$;

(2) $M \models P_{<s}\alpha \iff \mu([\alpha]) < s$;

(3) $M \models P_{>s}\alpha \iff \mu([\alpha]) > s$;

(4) $M \models P_{=s}\alpha \iff \mu([\alpha]) = s$.

Proof. (1)
$$M \models P_{\leq s}\alpha \overset{\text{S.E.}}{\iff} M \models P_{\geq 1-s}\neg\alpha \overset{\text{Definition 3.1.9}}{\iff}$$
$$\mu([\neg\alpha]) \geq 1-s \overset{\text{Remark 3.1.8}}{\iff}$$
$$1 - \mu([\alpha]) \geq 1 - s \iff \mu([\alpha]) \leq s \ .$$

(2) $M \models P_{<s}\alpha \overset{\text{S.E.}}{\Longleftrightarrow} M \models \neg P_{\geq s}\alpha \Longleftrightarrow M \not\models P_{\geq s}\alpha \overset{\text{Definition 3.1.9}}{\Longleftrightarrow} \mu([\alpha]) < s$.

(3) $M \models P_{>s}\alpha \overset{\text{S.E.}}{\Longleftrightarrow} M \models \neg P_{\leq s}\alpha \Longleftrightarrow M \not\models P_{\leq s}\alpha \overset{(1)}{\Longleftrightarrow} \mu([\alpha]) > s$.

(4)
$$M \models P_{=s}\alpha \overset{\text{S.E.}}{\Longleftrightarrow} M \models P_{\geq s}\alpha \wedge P_{\leq s}\alpha \Longleftrightarrow$$
$$\left(M \models P_{\geq s}\alpha \text{ and } M \models P_{\leq s}\alpha\right) \overset{(1) \text{ and Definition 3.1.9}}{\Longleftrightarrow}$$
$$\left(\mu([\alpha]) \geq s \text{ and } \mu([\alpha]) \leq s\right) \Longleftrightarrow \mu([\alpha]) = s \;. \qquad \square$$

3.2 Properties of the Logic PJ

In this section we establish some theorems that prove useful properties for the logic PJ.

First we have that the deduction theorem holds for the logic PJ.

Theorem 3.2.1 (Deduction Theorem for PJ)**.** *Let* $T \subseteq \mathcal{L}_{\mathsf{PJ}}$ *and assume that* $A, B \in \mathcal{L}_{\mathsf{PJ}}$. *Then for any* $\mathsf{PJ}_{\mathsf{CS}}$ *we have:*

$$T, A \vdash_{\mathsf{PJ}_{\mathsf{CS}}} B \Longleftrightarrow T \vdash_{\mathsf{PJ}_{\mathsf{CS}}} A \to B \;.$$

Proof. ($\Longleftarrow$): If $T \vdash_{\mathsf{PJ}_{\mathsf{CS}}} A \to B$ then we also have that $T, A \vdash_{\mathsf{PJ}_{\mathsf{CS}}} A \to B$ and trivially $T, A \vdash_{\mathsf{PJ}_{\mathsf{CS}}} A$. Thus by a simple application of (MP) we have $T, A \vdash_{\mathsf{PJ}_{\mathsf{CS}}} B$.

($\Longrightarrow$): By transfinite induction on the depth of the proof $T, A \vdash_{\mathsf{PJ}_{\mathsf{CS}}} B$. We distinguish cases depending on the last rule used to obtain B from T, A:

1. Assume that $B = A$. Then $A \to B$ is an instance of (P). Thus we trivially have $T \vdash_{\mathsf{PJ}_{\mathsf{CS}}} A \to B$.

2. Assume that $B \in T$ or B is an axiom of $\mathsf{PJ}_{\mathsf{CS}}$. Then $B \to (A \to B)$ is an instance of (P). Thus $T \vdash_{\mathsf{PJ}_{\mathsf{CS}}} B \to (A \to B)$. We also have that $T \vdash_{\mathsf{PJ}_{\mathsf{CS}}} B$. By an application of (MP) we get $T \vdash_{\mathsf{PJ}_{\mathsf{CS}}} A \to B$.

3. Assume that B is the result of an application of the rule (MP). That means there exists a C such that:
$$T, A \vdash_{\mathsf{PJ}_{\mathsf{CS}}} C$$
$$T, A \vdash_{\mathsf{PJ}_{\mathsf{CS}}} C \to B \;.$$

3.2. PROPERTIES OF THE LOGIC PJ

By the inductive hypothesis we get:

$$T \vdash_{\mathsf{PJ_{CS}}} A \to C$$
$$T \vdash_{\mathsf{PJ_{CS}}} A \to (C \to B) \ .$$

And by **P.R.** we have:

$$T \vdash_{\mathsf{PJ_{CS}}} A \to B \ .$$

4. Assume that B is the result of an application of (CE). That means there exists $\alpha \in \mathcal{L}_\mathsf{J}$ such that $B = P_{\geq 1}\alpha$ and also $\vdash_{\mathsf{J_{CS}}} \alpha$. Hence we have:

$\vdash_{\mathsf{J_{CS}}} \alpha$		(3.1)
$\vdash_{\mathsf{PJ_{CS}}} P_{\geq 1}\alpha$	[(3.1), (CE)]	(3.2)
$\vdash_{\mathsf{PJ_{CS}}} P_{\geq 1}\alpha \to (A \to P_{\geq 1}\alpha)$	[(P)]	(3.3)
$\vdash_{\mathsf{PJ_{CS}}} A \to P_{\geq 1}\alpha$	[(3.2), (3.3), (MP)]	
$T \vdash_{\mathsf{PJ_{CS}}} A \to B$.		

5. Assume that B is the result of an application of (ST). That means that $B = C \to P_{\geq s}\alpha$ and also for some positive $s \in \mathsf{S}$:

$$T, A \vdash_{\mathsf{PJ_{CS}}} C \to P_{\geq s-\frac{1}{k}}\alpha, \text{ for every integer } k \geq \frac{1}{s} \ .$$

Thus we have:

$T \vdash_{\mathsf{PJ_{CS}}} A \to (C \to P_{\geq s-\frac{1}{k}}\alpha)$, for every integer $k \geq \frac{1}{s}$	[i.h.]	(3.4)
$T \vdash_{\mathsf{PJ_{CS}}} (A \wedge C) \to P_{\geq s-\frac{1}{k}}\alpha$, for every integer $k \geq \frac{1}{s}$	[(3.4), **P.R.**]	(3.5)
$T \vdash_{\mathsf{PJ_{CS}}} (A \wedge C) \to P_{\geq s}\alpha$	[(3.5), (ST)]	(3.6)
$T \vdash_{\mathsf{PJ_{CS}}} A \to (C \to P_{\geq s}\alpha)$	[(3.6), **P.R.**]	(3.7)
$T \vdash_{\mathsf{PJ_{CS}}} A \to B$.	[(3.7), **S.E.**]	□

The following theorem states that if $\alpha \to \beta$ is a theorem of some $\mathsf{J_{CS}}$, then $\mathsf{PJ_{CS}}$ proves that β is at least as probable as α. It is interesting to observe that this property resembles the application axiom in modal and justification logics (and of course also the rule modus ponens). The theorem also states some monotonicity properties of inequalities that can be prove in $\mathsf{PJ_{CS}}$.

Lemma 3.2.2. *For any* $\mathsf{PJ_{CS}}$ *the following hold:*

(i) $\vdash_{\mathsf{PJ_{CS}}} P_{\geq 1}(\alpha \to \beta) \to (P_{\geq s}\alpha \to P_{\geq s}\beta)$;

(ii) If $\vdash_{\mathsf{J_{cs}}} \alpha \to \beta$ then $\vdash_{\mathsf{PJ_{cs}}} P_{\geq s}\alpha \to P_{\geq s}\beta$;

(iii) if $s > r$ then $\vdash_{\mathsf{PJ_{cs}}} P_{\geq s}\alpha \to P_{>r}\alpha$;

(iv) $\vdash_{\mathsf{PJ_{cs}}} P_{>r}\alpha \to P_{\geq r}\alpha$;

(v) if $r \geq s$ then $\vdash_{\mathsf{PJ_{cs}}} P_{\geq r}\alpha \to P_{\geq s}\alpha$.

Proof. All items are proved by purely syntactical arguments:

(i)

$\vdash_{\mathsf{J_{cs}}} \neg(\alpha \wedge \bot)$ [(P)]   (3.8)

$\vdash_{\mathsf{PJ_{cs}}} P_{\geq 1}\neg(\alpha \wedge \bot)$ [(3.8), (CE)]   (3.9)

$\vdash_{\mathsf{J_{cs}}} (\neg\alpha \wedge \neg\bot) \vee \neg\neg\alpha$ [(P)]   (3.10)

$\vdash_{\mathsf{PJ_{cs}}} P_{\geq 1}\big((\neg\alpha \wedge \neg\bot) \vee \neg\neg\alpha\big)$ [(3.10), (CE)]   (3.11)

$\vdash_{\mathsf{PJ_{cs}}} \big(P_{\geq s}\alpha \wedge P_{\geq 0}\bot \wedge P_{\geq 1}\neg(\alpha \wedge \bot)\big)$

     $\to P_{\geq s}(\alpha \vee \bot)$ [(DIS)]   (3.12)

$\vdash_{\mathsf{PJ_{cs}}} P_{\geq 0}\bot$ [(PI)]   (3.13)

$\vdash_{\mathsf{PJ_{cs}}} \big(P_{\geq s}\alpha \wedge P_{\geq 0}\bot\big) \to P_{\geq s}(\alpha \vee \bot)$ [(3.9), (3.12), **P.R.**]   (3.14)

$\vdash_{\mathsf{PJ_{cs}}} P_{\geq s}\alpha \to P_{\geq s}(\alpha \vee \bot)$ [(3.13), (3.14), **P.R.**]   (3.15)

$\vdash_{\mathsf{PJ_{cs}}} \big(P_{\leq 1-s}(\neg\alpha \wedge \neg\bot) \wedge P_{<s}\neg\neg\alpha\big)$

     $\to P_{<1}\big((\neg\alpha \wedge \neg\bot) \vee \neg\neg\alpha\big)$ (UN)   (3.16)

$\vdash_{\mathsf{PJ_{cs}}} \neg\neg P_{\geq 1}\big((\neg\alpha \wedge \neg\bot) \vee \neg\neg\alpha\big)$ [(3.11), **P.R.**]   (3.17)

$\vdash_{\mathsf{PJ_{cs}}} \neg P_{<1}\big((\neg\alpha \wedge \neg\bot) \vee \neg\neg\alpha\big)$ [(3.17), **S.E.**]   (3.18)

$\vdash_{\mathsf{PJ_{cs}}} \neg\big(P_{\leq 1-s}(\neg\alpha \wedge \neg\bot) \wedge P_{<s}\neg\neg\alpha\big)$ [(3.16), (3.18), **P.R.**]   (3.19)

$\vdash_{\mathsf{PJ_{cs}}} P_{\leq 1-s}(\neg\alpha \wedge \neg\bot) \to \neg P_{<s}\neg\neg\alpha$ [(3.19), **P.R.**]   (3.20)

$\vdash_{\mathsf{PJ_{cs}}} P_{\leq 1-s}(\neg\alpha \wedge \neg\bot) \to \neg\neg P_{\geq s}\neg\neg\alpha$ [(3.20), **S.E.**]   (3.21)

$\vdash_{\mathsf{PJ_{cs}}} P_{\leq 1-s}(\neg\alpha \wedge \neg\bot) \to P_{\geq s}\neg\neg\alpha$ [(3.21), **P.R.**]   (3.22)

$\vdash_{\mathsf{PJ_{cs}}} P_{\geq s}(\alpha \vee \bot) \to P_{\geq s}\neg\neg\alpha$ [(3.22), **S.E.**]   (3.23)

$\vdash_{\mathsf{PJ_{cs}}} P_{\geq s}\alpha \to P_{\geq s}\neg\neg\alpha$ [(3.15), (3.23), **P.R.**]   (3.24)

$\vdash_{\mathsf{PJ_{cs}}} \neg\big(P_{\geq 1}(\alpha \to \beta) \to (P_{\geq s}\alpha \to P_{\geq s}\beta)\big) \to$

     $P_{\geq 1}(\alpha \to \beta) \wedge P_{\geq s}\alpha \wedge \neg P_{\geq s}\beta$ [(P)]   (3.25)

$\vdash_{\mathsf{PJ_{cs}}} \neg\big(P_{\geq 1}(\alpha \to \beta) \to (P_{\geq s}\alpha \to P_{\geq s}\beta)\big) \to$

3.2. PROPERTIES OF THE LOGIC PJ

$$P_{\geq 1}(\alpha \to \beta) \wedge P_{\geq s}\neg\neg\alpha \wedge \neg P_{\geq s}\beta \qquad [(3.24),(3.25),\textbf{P.R.}] \quad (3.26)$$

$$\vdash_{\mathsf{PJ_{cs}}} \neg\bigl(P_{\geq 1}(\alpha \to \beta) \to (P_{\geq s}\alpha \to P_{\geq s}\beta)\bigr) \to$$
$$P_{\geq 1}(\neg\alpha \vee \beta) \wedge P_{\leq 1-s}\neg\alpha \wedge P_{<s}\beta \qquad [(3.26),\textbf{S.E.}] \quad (3.27)$$

$$\vdash_{\mathsf{PJ_{cs}}} P_{\leq 1-s}\neg\alpha \wedge P_{<s}\beta \to P_{<1}(\neg\alpha \vee \beta) \qquad [(\text{UN})] \quad (3.28)$$

$$\vdash_{\mathsf{PJ_{cs}}} \neg\bigl(P_{\geq 1}(\alpha \to \beta) \to (P_{\geq s}\alpha \to P_{\geq s}\beta)\bigr) \to$$
$$\bigl(P_{\geq 1}(\neg\alpha \vee \beta) \wedge P_{<1}(\neg\alpha \vee \beta)\bigr) \qquad [(3.27),(3.28),\textbf{P.R.}] \quad (3.29)$$

$$\vdash_{\mathsf{PJ_{cs}}} \neg\bigl(P_{\geq 1}(\alpha \to \beta) \to (P_{\geq s}\alpha \to P_{\geq s}\beta)\bigr) \to$$
$$\bigl(P_{\geq 1}(\neg\alpha \vee \beta) \wedge \neg P_{\geq 1}(\neg\alpha \vee \beta)\bigr) \qquad [(3.29),\textbf{S.E.}] \quad (3.30)$$

$$\vdash_{\mathsf{PJ_{cs}}} P_{\geq 1}(\alpha \to \beta) \to (P_{\geq s}\alpha \to P_{\geq s}\beta). \qquad [(3.30),\textbf{P.R.}]$$

(ii)
$$\vdash_{\mathsf{J_{cs}}} \alpha \to \beta \qquad (3.31)$$
$$\vdash_{\mathsf{PJ_{cs}}} P_{\geq 1}(\alpha \to \beta) \qquad [(3.31),(\text{CE})] \quad (3.32)$$
$$\vdash_{\mathsf{PJ_{cs}}} P_{\geq 1}(\alpha \to \beta) \to (P_{\geq s}\alpha \to P_{\geq s}\beta) \qquad [(i)] \quad (3.33)$$
$$\vdash_{\mathsf{PJ_{cs}}} P_{\geq s}\alpha \to P_{\geq s}\beta. \qquad [(3.32),(3.33),(\text{MP})]$$

(iii)
$$\vdash_{\mathsf{PJ_{cs}}} P_{\leq r}\alpha \to P_{<s}\alpha \qquad [(\text{WE})] \quad (3.34)$$
$$\vdash_{\mathsf{PJ_{cs}}} \neg P_{<s}\alpha \to \neg P_{\leq r}\alpha \qquad [(3.34),\textbf{P.R.}] \quad (3.35)$$
$$\vdash_{\mathsf{PJ_{cs}}} \neg\neg P_{\geq s}\alpha \to P_{>r}\alpha \qquad [(3.35),\textbf{S.E.}] \quad (3.36)$$
$$\vdash_{\mathsf{PJ_{cs}}} P_{\geq s}\alpha \to P_{>r}\alpha. \qquad [(3.36),\textbf{P.R.}]$$

(iv)
$$\vdash_{\mathsf{PJ_{cs}}} P_{<r}\alpha \to P_{\leq r}\alpha \qquad [(\text{LE})] \quad (3.37)$$
$$\vdash_{\mathsf{PJ_{cs}}} \neg P_{\leq r}\alpha \to \neg P_{<r}\alpha \qquad [(3.37),\textbf{P.R.}] \quad (3.38)$$
$$\vdash_{\mathsf{PJ_{cs}}} P_{>r}\alpha \to \neg\neg P_{\geq r}\alpha \qquad [(3.38),\textbf{S.E.}] \quad (3.39)$$
$$\vdash_{\mathsf{PJ_{cs}}} P_{>r}\alpha \to P_{\geq r}\alpha. \qquad [(3.39),\textbf{P.R.}]$$

(v) If $r = s$ then we have that $P_{\geq r}\alpha \to P_{\geq s}\alpha$ is an instance of (P). If $r > s$ we have the following:

$$\vdash_{\mathsf{PJ_{cs}}} P_{\geq r}\alpha \to P_{>s}\alpha \qquad [(iii)] \quad (3.40)$$
$$\vdash_{\mathsf{PJ_{cs}}} P_{>s}\alpha \to P_{\geq s}\alpha \qquad [(iv)] \quad (3.41)$$
$$\vdash_{\mathsf{PJ_{cs}}} P_{\geq r}\alpha \to P_{\geq s}\alpha. \qquad [(3.40),(3.41),\textbf{P.R.}] \quad \square$$

Internalization states that the logic internalizes the notion of its own proof, i.e. when we have a proof in a logic, then a formula that "encodes" this proof is provable in the logic. In probabilistic internalization we have the same property, but with a form of uncertainty in the premises. Many forms of probabilistic internalization can be proved for the logic PJ. Theorem 3.2.3 states two of them. Item (1) of Theorem 3.2.3 states that if we have uncertainty for the conjunction of the premises, this uncertainty is passed to the result, whereas item (2) of Theorem 3.2.3 states that uncertainty in a single premise is again passed to the result.

Theorem 3.2.3 (Probabilistic Internalization). *Let CS be an axiomatically appropriate constant specification for the logic J. For any $\alpha, \beta_1, \ldots, \beta_n \in \mathcal{L}_J$, $t_1, \ldots, t_n \in \mathsf{Tm}$ and $s \in \mathsf{S}$, if:*

$$\beta_1, \ldots, \beta_n \vdash_{\mathsf{Jcs}} \alpha$$

then there exists a term t such that:

(1) $P_{\geq s}(t_1 : \beta_1 \wedge \ldots \wedge t_n : \beta_n) \vdash_{\mathsf{PJcs}} P_{\geq s}(t : \alpha)$;

(2) *for every $i \in \{1, \ldots, n\}$:*

$$\left\{ P_{\geq 1}(t_j : \beta_j) \;\middle|\; j \neq i \right\}, P_{\geq s}(t_i : \beta_i) \vdash_{\mathsf{PJcs}} P_{\geq s}(t : \alpha) .$$

Proof. By Theorem 2.3.1 we find that there exists a term t such that:

$$t_1 : \beta_1, \ldots, t_n : \beta_n \vdash_{\mathsf{Jcs}} t : \alpha .$$

By repeatedly applying Theorem 2.3.2 we get:

$$\vdash_{\mathsf{Jcs}} t_1 : \beta_1 \to (\ldots \to (t_{n-1} : \beta_{n-1} \to (t_n : \beta_n \to t : \alpha)) \ldots) . \tag{3.42}$$

So we have:

(1) By statement (3.42) and **P.R.** we get:

$$\vdash_{\mathsf{Jcs}} \left(t_1 : \beta_1 \wedge \ldots \wedge t_n : \beta_n\right) \to t : \alpha .$$

By Lemma 3.2.2(ii):

$$\vdash_{\mathsf{PJcs}} P_{\geq s}\left(t_1 : \beta_1 \wedge \ldots \wedge t_n : \beta_n\right) \to P_{\geq s}\left(t : \alpha\right)$$

and by Theorem 3.2.1:

$$P_{\geq s}\left(t_1 : \beta_1 \wedge \ldots \wedge t_n : \beta_n\right) \vdash_{\mathsf{PJcs}} P_{\geq s}\left(t : \alpha\right) .$$

(2) Let $i \in \{1, \ldots, n\}$ and $\{j_1, \ldots, j_{n-1}\} = \{1, \ldots, n\} \setminus i$. By statement (3.42) and **P.R.** we get:

$$\vdash_{\mathsf{Jcs}} t_{j_1} : \beta_{j_1} \to (\ldots \to (t_{j_{n-1}} : \beta_{j_{n-1}} \to (t_i : \beta_i \to t : \alpha)) \ldots) .$$

3.2. PROPERTIES OF THE LOGIC PJ

By (CE) we get:

$$\vdash_{\mathsf{PJ_{CS}}} P_{\geq 1}\Big(t_{j_1} : \beta_{j_1} \to (\ \ldots\ \to (t_{j_{n-1}} : \beta_{j_{n-1}} \to (t_i : \beta_i \to t : \alpha))\ldots)\Big).$$

By repeatedly applying Lemma 3.2.2(i) and **P.R.** we get:

$$\vdash_{\mathsf{PJ_{CS}}} P_{\geq 1}(t_{j_1} : \beta_{j_1}) \to (\ \ldots\ \to (P_{\geq 1}(t_{j_{n-1}} : \beta_{j_{n-1}}) \to (P_{\geq s}(t_i : \beta_i) \to P_{\geq s}(t : \alpha)))\ldots).$$

And by repeatedly applying Theorem 3.2.1 we get:

$$P_{\geq 1}\big(t_{j_1} : \beta_{j_1}\big),\ \ldots\ ,P_{\geq 1}\big(t_{j_{n-1}} : \beta_{j_{n-1}}\big), P_{\geq s}\big(t_i : \beta_i\big) \vdash_{\mathsf{PJ_{CS}}} P_{\geq s}\big(t : \alpha\big)$$

i.e.

$$\big\{\, P_{\geq 1}(t_j : \beta_j) \ \big|\ j \neq i\, \big\}, P_{\geq s}(t_i : \beta_i) \vdash_{\mathsf{PJ_{CS}}} P_{\geq s}(t : \alpha)\,. \qquad \square$$

Remark 3.2.4. If we consider the formulation of probabilistic internalization without premises, then for an axiomatically appropriate CS we obtain that:

$$\vdash_{\mathsf{J_{CS}}} \alpha \qquad \text{implies} \qquad \vdash_{\mathsf{PJ_{CS}}} P_{\geq 1}(t : \alpha) \quad \text{for some term } t.$$

The above rule contains a combination of constructive and probabilistic necessitation.

We close this section by presenting a semantical characterization of independence in the system PJ. It seems that a syntactical characterization of independence is impossible in PJ.

Theorem 3.2.5. *Let* CS *be a constant specification for the logic* J. *Let* $u, v \in \mathsf{Tm}$, *let* $\alpha, \beta \in \mathcal{L}_\mathsf{J}$ *and let* M *be a* $\mathsf{PJ_{CS,Meas}}$-*model. Assume that* $[u : (\alpha \to \beta)]_M$ *and* $[v : \alpha]_M$ *are independent in* M. *Then for any* $r, s \in \mathsf{S}$ *we have:*

$$M \models P_{\geq r}(u : (\alpha \to \beta)) \to \Big(P_{\geq s}(v : \alpha) \to P_{\geq r \cdot s}(u \cdot v : \beta)\Big).$$

Proof. Assume that $M = \langle W, H, \mu, * \rangle$.

Let $w \in [u : (\alpha \to \beta)] \cap [v : \alpha]$. We have that $*_w \models u : (\alpha \to \beta)$ and that $*_w \models v : \alpha$. Since $*_w$ is a CS-evaluation, by Theorem 2.3.3 we get that $*_w$ satisfies all instances of axiom (J), i.e. $*_w \models u : (\alpha \to \beta) \to (v : \alpha \to u \cdot v : \beta)$. Hence we have $*_w \models u \cdot v : \beta$, i.e. $w \in [u \cdot v : \beta]$. So we proved that $[u : (\alpha \to \beta)] \cap [v : \alpha] \subseteq [u \cdot v : \beta]$. So by Lemma 3.1.7(3) we get:

$$\mu\big([u \cdot v : \beta]\big) \geq \mu\big([u : (\alpha \to \beta)] \cap [v : \alpha]\big).$$

And since $[u : (\alpha \to \beta)]$ and $[v : \alpha]$ are independent in M we have:

$$\mu\big([u \cdot v : \beta]\big) \geq \mu\big([u : (\alpha \to \beta)]\big) \cdot \mu\big([v : \alpha]\big). \tag{3.43}$$

Assume that:

$$M \models P_{\geq r}(u:(\alpha \to \beta)) \text{ and } M \models P_{\geq s}(v:\alpha), \text{ i.e.}$$
$$\mu\Big([u:(\alpha \to \beta)]\Big) \geq r \text{ and } \mu\Big([v:\alpha]\Big) \geq s .$$

By inequality (3.43) we have $\mu\big([u \cdot v : \beta]\big) \geq r \cdot s$, i.e. $M \models P_{\geq r \cdot s}(u \cdot v : \beta)$. Hence we proved that:

$$M \models P_{\geq r}(u:(\alpha \to \beta)) \to \Big(P_{\geq s}(v:\alpha) \to P_{\geq r \cdot s}(u \cdot v : \beta)\Big) . \qquad \square$$

3.3 The Probabilistic Justification Logic PPJ

Observe that the language of PJ does neither include justification operators over probability operators (e.g. $t : (P_{\geq s} A)$) nor iterations of the probability operator (e.g. $P_{\geq r}(P_{\geq s} A)$). In this section, we present a logic over a language that remedies these shortcomings. The logic PPJ [KOS16] allows formulas of the form $t : (P_{\geq s} A)$ as well as $P_{\geq r}(P_{\geq s} A)$. This explains the name PPJ: the two P's refer to iterated P-operators. Since we can have justification over probabilities it is possible to extend the notion of constant specification. A constant specification for the logic PPJ will contain instances of the justification as well as the probabilistic axioms (see Figure 3.3.1).

Syntax

The language $\mathcal{L}_{\mathsf{PPJ}}$ is defined by the following grammar:

$$A ::= p \mid P_{\geq s} A \mid \neg A \mid A \wedge A \mid t : A$$

where $t \in \mathsf{Tm}, s \in \mathsf{S}$ and $p \in \mathsf{Prop}$. For the language $\mathcal{L}_{\mathsf{PPJ}}$ we assume the same abbreviations as for the language $\mathcal{L}_{\mathsf{PJ}}$.

The axiom schemata of the logic PPJ are presented in Figure 3.3.1.

Let CS be any constant specification for the logic PPJ. The deductive system PPJ$_{\mathsf{CS}}$ is the Hilbert system obtained by adding to the axiom schemata of PPJ the rules (MP), (CE), (ST) and (AN!) as given in Figure 3.3.2.

As we can see, the axiomatization for PPJ$_{\mathsf{CS}}$ is simply a combination of the axiomatization for PJ$_{\mathsf{CS}}$ and the axiomatization for J$_{\mathsf{CS}}$. However, the version of rule (CE) that is used for the logic PPJ deserves some comment. As the reader can recall, rule (CE) has also been used in the axiomatization of the logic PJ, with different condition on the premise: when we have $\vdash_{\mathsf{J}_{\mathsf{CS}}} \alpha$, then we can prove $\vdash_{\mathsf{PJ}_{\mathsf{CS}}} P_{\geq 1}\alpha$. The reason why formula α has to be a theorem of J$_{\mathsf{CS}}$ is clear since the premise

3.3. THE PROBABILISTIC JUSTIFICATION LOGIC PPJ

(P)		finitely many axiom schemata in the language of $\mathcal{L}_{\mathsf{PPJ}}$ axiomatizing classical propositional logic
(J)		$\vdash u : (A \to B) \to (v : A \to u \cdot v : B)$
(+)		$(\vdash u : A \vee v : A) \to u + v : A$
(PI)		$\vdash P_{\geq 0} A$
(WE)		$\vdash P_{\leq r} A \to P_{<s} A$, where $s > r$
(LE)		$\vdash P_{<s} A \to P_{\leq s} A$
(DIS)		$\vdash P_{\geq r} A \wedge P_{\geq s} B \wedge P_{\geq 1} \neg (A \wedge B) \to P_{\geq \min(1, r+s)}(A \vee B)$
(UN)		$\vdash P_{\leq r} A \wedge P_{<s} B \to P_{<r+s}(A \vee B)$, where $r + s \leq 1$

Figure 3.3.1: Axiom Schemata of PPJ

	axiom schemata of PPJ
	+
(AN!)	$\vdash !^n c : !^{n-1} c : \cdots : !c : c : A$, where $(c, A) \in \mathsf{CS}$ and $n \in \mathbb{N}$
(MP)	if $T \vdash A$ and $T \vdash A \to B$ then $T \vdash B$
(CE)	if $\vdash A$ then $\vdash P_{\geq 1} A$
(ST)	if $T \vdash A \to P_{\geq s - \frac{1}{k}} B$ for every integer $k \geq \frac{1}{s}$ and $s > 0$ then $T \vdash A \to P_{\geq s} B$

Figure 3.3.2: System $\mathsf{PPJ_{CS}}$

of the rule is proved in a different logic than the result of the rule. In the case of PPJ one could argue that rule (CE) could be formulated without the condition that the premise is a theorem, since there is only one logical system (the system PPJ) involved. However, it turns out the Deduction Theorem (Theorem 3.3.9) cannot be proved without this condition. That is why we have the condition that the premise of the rule (CE) is a theorem in PPJ.

Semantics

A $\mathsf{PPJ_{CS}}$-model is a combination of a $\mathsf{PJ_{CS}}$-model and a $\mathsf{J_{CS}}$-model. It consists of a probability space, where to every possible world a CS- evaluation as well as a probability space is assigned. This way we can deal with iterated probabilities and justifications over probabilities.

We proceed by formally defining the notion of a $\mathsf{PPJ_{CS}}$-model and the notion of satisfiability in PPJ$_{CS}$-models.

Definition 3.3.1 (PPJ$_{CS}$-Model). Let CS be a constant specification for the logic PPJ. A PPJ$_{CS}$-*model* is a quintuple $M = \langle U, W, H, \mu, * \rangle$ where:

1. U is a non-empty set of objects called worlds;

2. W, H, μ and $*$ are functions, which have U as their domain, such that for every $w \in U$:

   - $\langle W(w), H(w), \mu(w) \rangle$ is a probability space with $W(w) \subseteq U$;
   - $*_w$ is a CS-evaluation[1].

The ternary satisfaction relation $\models$ is defined between models, worlds, and formulas.

Definition 3.3.2 (Truth in a PPJ$_{CS}$-model). Let CS be a constant specification for the logic PPJ and let $M = \langle U, W, H, \mu, * \rangle$ be a PPJ$_{CS}$-model. We define what it means for an $\mathcal{L}_{PPJ}$-formula to hold in M at a world $w \in U$ inductively as follows:

$$
\begin{aligned}
M, w \models p & \iff p_w^* = \mathsf{T} \quad \text{for } p \in \mathsf{Prop} ; \\
M, w \models P_{\geq s} B & \iff \Big([B]_{M,w} \in H(w) \text{ and } \mu(w)\big([B]_{M,w}\big) \geq s \Big) \\
& \qquad \text{where } [B]_{M,w} = \{x \in W(w) \mid M, x \models B\} ; \\
M, w \models \neg B & \iff M, w \not\models B ; \\
M, w \models B \wedge C & \iff \Big(M, w \models B \text{ and } M, w \models C \Big) ; \\
M, w \models t : B & \iff B \in t_w^* .
\end{aligned}
$$

Measurable models are defined as expected.

Definition 3.3.3 (Measurable Model). Let CS be a constant specification for the logic PPJ and let $M = \langle U, W, H, \mu, * \rangle$ be a PPJ$_{CS}$-model. M is called measurable iff for every $w \in U$ and for every $A \in \mathcal{L}_{PPJ}$:

$$[A]_{M,w} \in H(w) .$$

PPJ$_{CS,Meas}$ denotes the class of PPJ$_{CS}$-measurable models.

---
[1] We will usually write $*_w$ instead of $*(w)$.

3.3. THE PROBABILISTIC JUSTIFICATION LOGIC PPJ

Remark 3.3.4. In Definition 3.3.2, the condition for the truth of $P_{\geq s}B$ may have some "strange" consequences. For example, we may have $M, w \models \neg P_{\geq s}B$ when $[B]_{M,w} \notin H(w)$. However, this condition becomes "normal" for measurable models, i.e. for a measurable model $M = \langle U, W, H, \mu, * \rangle$ we have:

$$M, w \models P_{\geq s}B \iff \mu(w)\big([B]_{M,w}\big) \geq s \ .$$

Since we are going to use only measurable models, the "strange" consequences of Definition 3.3.2 will not be important for us.

Definition 3.3.5 (Semantical Consequence and Satisfiability in PPJ). Let T be a subset of $\mathcal{L}_{\mathsf{PPJ}}$, let $A \in \mathcal{L}_{\mathsf{PPJ}}$ and let $M = \langle U, W, H, \mu, * \rangle$ be a $\mathsf{PPJ}_{\mathsf{CS,Meas}}$-model.

- We say that A is *satisfied in the world* $w \in U$ iff $M, w \models A$.

- We say that A is *satisfied in the model* M iff there is a world $w \in U$, such that $M, w \models A$.

- We say that A is $\mathsf{PPJ}_{\mathsf{CS,Meas}}$-*satisfiable* (or simply satisfiable, if there is no danger of confusion) iff there exists a $\mathsf{PPJ}_{\mathsf{CS,Meas}}$-model where A is satisfied.

- We write $M, w \models T$ if and only if:

$$(\forall A \in T)\big[M, w \models A\big] \ .$$

- We say that A is a semantical consequence of T (we write $T \models_{\mathsf{PPJ}_{\mathsf{CS,Meas}}} A$) iff for every $\mathsf{PPJ}_{\mathsf{CS,Meas}}$-model M and for for every world w of M:

$$M, w \models T \implies M, w \models A \ .$$

Remark 3.3.6. Let $T \subseteq \mathsf{PPJ}$, let $A \in \mathsf{PPJ}$ and let M be some $\mathsf{PPJ}_{\mathsf{CS,Meas}}$-model. The notion of semantical consequence defined in Definition 3.3.5 is usually called *local* semantical consequence, since it is required that A holds in some world of M if T holds in the same world of M. A notion of *global* semantical consequence can also be defined, where, given some model M, A has to hold in all worlds of M, if T holds in all worlds of M. However, in this thesis we will use only the notion of local semantical consequence.

We now define two important decision problems that are related to the logic PJ.

Definition 3.3.7 (The $\mathsf{PPJ}_{\mathsf{CS,Meas}}$-Satisfiability Problem). Let CS be any constant specification for the logic PPJ. The $\mathsf{PPJ}_{\mathsf{CS,Meas}}$-satisfiability problem is the following decision problem:

for a given $A \in \mathcal{L}_{PPJ}$ is A $PPJ_{CS,Meas}$-satisfiable?

Definition 3.3.8 (The PPJ_{CS}-Derivability Problem). Let CS be any constant specification for the logic PPJ. The PPJ_{CS}-derivability problem or the derivability problem in the logic J_{CS} is the following decision problem:

for a given $A \in \mathcal{L}_{PPJ}$, is there a proof for A in PPJ_{CS}?

Finally we have the deduction theorem for PPJ. Its proof is almost identical with the proof of the deduction theorem for the logic PJ. The only modifications concern the justification axioms and the rule (AN!) that belong to the axiomatics of PPJ and not to the axiomatics of PJ. However, these modifications are trivial, thus we present the deduction theorem for PPJ without a proof.

Theorem 3.3.9 (Deduction Theorem for PPJ). *Let* $T \subseteq \mathcal{L}_{PPJ}$ *and* $A, B \in \mathcal{L}_{PPJ}$. *For any* PPJ_{CS} *we have:*

$$T, A \vdash_{PPJ_{CS}} B \iff T \vdash_{PPJ_{CS}} A \to B .$$

3.4 Application to the Lottery Paradox

Kyburg's famous lottery paradox [Kyb61] goes as follows. Consider a fair lottery with 1000 tickets that has exactly one winning ticket. Now assume a proposition is believed if and only if its degree of belief is greater than 0.99. In this setting it is rational to believe that ticket 1 does not win, it is rational to believe that ticket 2 does not win, and so on. However, this entails that it is rational to believe that no ticket wins because rational belief is closed under conjunction. Hence it is rational to believe that no ticket wins and that one ticket wins.

PPJ_{CS} makes the following analysis of the lottery paradox possible. First we need a principle to move from degrees of belief to rational belief (this formalizes what Foley [Fol09] calls *the Lockean thesis*): we suppose that for each term t, there exists a term $pb(t)$ such that:

$$t : (P_{>0.99}A) \to pb(t) : A . \quad (3.44)$$

Let w_i be the proposition *ticket i wins*. For each $1 \leq i \leq 1000$, there is a term t_i such that $t_i : \left(P_{=\frac{999}{1000}} \neg w_i\right)$ holds. Hence by statement (3.44) we get

$$pb(t_i) : \neg w_i \quad \text{for each } 1 \leq i \leq 1000. \quad (3.45)$$

3.4. APPLICATION TO THE LOTTERY PARADOX

Now if CS is an axiomatically appropriate constant specification for PPJ, then

$$s_1 : A \wedge s_2 : B \to \mathsf{con}(s_1, s_2) : (A \wedge B) \qquad (3.46)$$

is a valid principle (for a suitable term $\mathsf{con}(s_1, s_2)$) in the semantics of $\mathsf{PPJ_{CS}}$. Hence by statement (3.45) we conclude that

$$\text{there exists a term } t \text{ with } t : (\neg w_1 \wedge \cdots \wedge \neg w_{1000}) \ , \qquad (3.47)$$

which leads to a paradoxical situation since it is also believed that one of the tickets wins.

In $\mathsf{PPJ_{CS}}$ we can resolve this problem by restricting the constant specification such that (3.46) is valid only if $\mathsf{con}(s_1, s_2)$ does not contain two different subterms of the form $\mathsf{pb}(t)$. Then the step from (3.45) to (3.47) is no longer possible and we can avoid the paradoxical belief.

This analysis is inspired by Leitgeb's [Lei14] solution to the lottery paradox and his *Stability Theory of Belief* according to which *it is not permissible to apply the conjunction rule for beliefs across different contexts.* Our proposed restriction of (3.46) is one way to achieve this in a formal system. A related and very interesting question is whether one can interpret the above justifications t_i as stable sets in Leitgeb's sense. Of course, our discussion of the lottery paradox is very sketchy but we think that probabilistic justification logic provides a promising approach to it that is worth further investigations.

Chapter 4

Soundness and Completeness

In this chapter we present soundness and strong completeness theorems for the logics PJ and PPJ. The soundness theorems (in Section 4.1) are proved by a transfinite induction on the depth of the proof. The strong completeness theorems (in Sections 4.2 and 4.3) are obtained by applying the standard Henkin procedure.

4.1 Soundness

In order to prove the soundness theorems we need the Archimedean property for the real numbers.

Proposition 4.1.1 (Archimedean Property for the Real Numbers). *For any real number $\epsilon > 0$ there exists an $n \in \mathbb{N}$ such that $\frac{1}{n} < \epsilon$.*

The following theorem states that any $\mathsf{PJ_{CS}}$ is sound with respect to the class $\mathsf{PJ_{CS,Meas}}$.

Theorem 4.1.2 (Soundness for PJ). *Let $T \subseteq \mathcal{L}_{\mathsf{PJ}}$ and let $A \in \mathcal{L}_{\mathsf{PJ}}$. Then for any constant specification CS for the logic J we have:*

$$T \vdash_{\mathsf{PJ_{CS}}} A \implies T \models_{\mathsf{PJ_{CS,Meas}}} A \ .$$

Proof. Let $T \subseteq \mathcal{L}_{\mathsf{PJ}}$ and let $A \in \mathcal{L}_{\mathsf{PJ}}$. We prove the claim by transfinite induction on the depth of the derivation $T \vdash_{\mathsf{PJ_{CS}}} A$. Let $M = \langle W, H, \mu, * \rangle \in \mathsf{PJ_{CS,Meas}}$. We assume that $M \models T$. We distinguish the following cases:

(1) $A \in T$. Then M satisfies A by assumption.

(2) A is an instance of (P). Then obviously M satisfies A.

(3) A is an instance of (PI). This means:
$$A = P_{\geq 0}\alpha .$$

Since $\mu : H \to [0,1]$ and $[\alpha] \in H$ we have $\mu([\alpha]) \geq 0$, i.e. $M \models P_{\geq 0}\alpha$, i.e. $M \models A$.

(4) A is an instance of (WE). That means:
$$A = P_{\leq r}\alpha \to P_{<s}\alpha, \text{ with } s > r .$$

We have:
$$M \models A \quad\Longleftrightarrow$$
$$\left(M \models P_{\leq r}\alpha \Longrightarrow M \models P_{<s}\alpha\right) \quad\overset{\text{Lemma 3.1.13(2)}}{\Longleftrightarrow}$$
$$\left(\mu([\alpha]) \leq r \Longrightarrow \mu([\alpha]) < s\right)$$

The last statement is true since $r < s$. Thus $M \models A$.

(5) A is an instance of (LE). Similar to case (4).

(6) A is an instance of (DIS). Then we have:
$$A = \left(P_{\geq r}\alpha \wedge P_{\geq s}\beta \wedge P_{\geq 1}\neg(\alpha \wedge \beta)\right) \to P_{\geq \min(1,r+s)}(\alpha \vee \beta) .$$

It holds:
$$M \models A \quad\Longleftrightarrow$$
$$M \models \left(P_{\geq r}\alpha \wedge P_{\geq s}\beta \wedge P_{\geq 1}\neg(\alpha \wedge \beta)\right) \to P_{\geq \min(1,r+s)}(\alpha \vee \beta) \quad\overset{\text{S.E.}}{\Longleftrightarrow}$$
$$M \models \left(P_{\geq r}\alpha \wedge P_{\geq s}\beta \wedge P_{\leq 0}(\alpha \wedge \beta)\right) \to P_{\geq \min(1,r+s)}(\alpha \vee \beta) .$$

By Lemma 3.1.13(2) the last statement is equivalent to:
$$\left(\mu([\alpha]) \geq r \text{ and } \mu([\beta]) \geq s \text{ and } \mu([\alpha \wedge \beta]) \leq 0\right) \Longrightarrow$$
$$\mu([\alpha \vee \beta]) \geq \min(1, r + s) .$$

Let $\mu([\alpha]) \geq r$, $\mu([\beta]) \geq s$ and $\mu([\alpha \wedge \beta]) \leq 0$. By Remark 3.1.8 we have: $\mu([\alpha \vee \beta]) = \mu([\alpha]) + \mu([\beta]) - \mu([\alpha \wedge \beta]) \geq r + s$. Since $\mu([\alpha \vee \beta]) \leq 1$ we have $\mu([\alpha \vee \beta]) \geq \min(1, r + s)$. Thus, the last of the above statements is true, so $M \models A$.

4.1. SOUNDNESS

(7) A is an instance of (UN). Then we have:
$$A = \left(P_{\leq r}\alpha \land P_{<s}\beta\right) \to P_{<r+s}(\alpha \lor \beta),\ r+s \leq 1\ .$$

We have:
$$M \models A \iff$$
$$\left(M \models \left(P_{\leq r}\alpha \land P_{<s}\beta\right) \to P_{<r+s}(\alpha \lor \beta)\right) \stackrel{\text{Lemma 3.1.13}}{\iff}$$
$$\left(\left(\mu([\alpha]) \leq r \text{ and } \mu([\beta]) < s\right) \implies \mu([\alpha \lor \beta]) < r+s\right)\ .$$

Assume that $\mu([\alpha]) \leq r$ and $\mu([\beta]) < s$. By Remark 3.1.8 we have that $\mu([\alpha \lor \beta]) = \mu([\alpha]) + \mu([\beta]) - \mu([\alpha \land \beta]) < r+s - \mu([\alpha \land \beta])$. Since $\mu([\alpha \land \beta]) \geq 0$ we have $\mu([\alpha \lor \beta]) < r+s$. Thus, the last of the above statements is true, so $M \models A$.

(8) A is obtained by an application of the rule (MP). Thus, there exists some $B \in \mathcal{L}_{\text{PJ}}$ such that $T \vdash_{\text{PJ}_{\text{CS}}} B$ and $T \vdash_{\text{PJ}_{\text{CS}}} B \to A$. By the inductive hypothesis we have that $M \models B$ and $M \models B \to A$. Thus $M \models A$.

(9) A is obtained by an application of the rule (CE). That means $A = P_{\geq 1}\alpha$ and also $\vdash_{\text{J}_{\text{CS}}} \alpha$ for some $\alpha \in \mathcal{L}_{\text{J}}$. By Theorem 2.3.3 we have $\models_{\text{CS}} \alpha$, which implies that $(\forall w \in W)[*_w \models \alpha]$, i.e. $[\alpha] = W$. Thus $\mu([\alpha]) = 1$, i.e. $M \models P_{\geq 1}\alpha$.

(10) A is obtained by an application of (ST). That means $A = B \to P_{\geq s}\beta$ for $s > 0$ and also $T \vdash_{\text{PJ}_{\text{CS}}} B \to P_{\geq s - \frac{1}{k}}\beta$ for every integer $k \geq \frac{1}{s}$. By the inductive hypothesis we have that $M \models B \to P_{\geq s - \frac{1}{k}}\beta$ for every integer $k \geq \frac{1}{s}$.

Assume that $M \models B$. This implies that for every integer $k \geq \frac{1}{s}$ we have $M \models P_{\geq s - \frac{1}{k}}\beta$, i.e.

$$\mu([\beta]) \geq s - \frac{1}{k} \qquad \text{for every integer } k \geq \frac{1}{s}. \tag{4.1}$$

Assume that $\mu([\beta]) < s$, i.e. $s - \mu([\beta]) > 0$. By the Archimedean property for the real numbers we know that there exists some integer n such that $\frac{1}{n} < s - \mu([\beta])$, which implies $n > \frac{1}{s - \mu([\beta])} \geq \frac{1}{s}$ since $s > \mu([\beta]) \geq 0$. Hence, there exists some $n \geq \frac{1}{s}$ with $\mu([\beta]) < s - \frac{1}{n}$, which contradicts (4.1). Thus $\mu([\beta]) \geq s$, i.e. $M \models P_{\geq s}\beta$. So, we proved that $M \models B$ implies $M \models P_{\geq s}\beta$. As a consequence we have that $M \models A$. □

In a very similar way we can prove that any PPJ_{CS} is sound with respect to the class $\text{PPJ}_{\text{CS,Meas}}$.

Theorem 4.1.3 (Soundness for PPJ)**.** *Let* CS *be any constant specification for the logic* PPJ*. Then the following holds:*

$$(\forall A \in \mathcal{L}_{\mathsf{PPJ}})(\forall T \subseteq \mathcal{L}_{\mathsf{PPJ}})\big[T \vdash_{\mathsf{PPJ}_{\mathsf{CS}}} A \implies T \models_{\mathsf{PPJ}_{\mathsf{CS}}} A\big] \ .$$

Proof. Let $A \in \mathcal{L}_{\mathsf{PPJ}}$. Then our goal is to show the following statement:

$$(\forall T \subseteq \mathcal{L}_{\mathsf{PPJ}})\big[T \vdash_{\mathsf{PPJ}_{\mathsf{CS}}} A \implies T \models_{\mathsf{PPJ}_{\mathsf{CS}}} A\big] \ .$$

The proof is done by transfinite induction on the depth of the $\mathsf{PPJ}_{\mathsf{CS}}$-derivation for A. Since the cases for the probabilistic axioms and rules are similar to the ones from Theorem 4.1.2, here we show only the cases for the justification axioms and rules plus the case for the rule (CE) which is slightly different:

- A is an instance of (J). That means:

$$A \equiv u : (B \to C) \to (v : B \to u \cdot v : C) \ .$$

Let

$$M = \langle U, W, H, \mu, * \rangle \in \mathsf{PPJ}_{\mathsf{CS},\mathsf{Meas}}$$

and let $w \in U$ be such that $M, w \models T$. Our goal is to show that $M, w \models A$. The following statements are equivalent:

$$M, w \models A$$
$$M, w \models u : (B \to C) \to (v : B \to u \cdot v : C)$$
$$\big[\big(M, w \models u : B \to C\big) \text{ and } \big(M, w \models v : B\big)\big] \implies M, w \models u \cdot v : C$$
$$\big(B \to C \in u_w^*\big) \text{ and } \big(B \in v_w^*\big) \implies C \in (u \cdot v)_w^* \ .$$

The last statement is true according to Definition 2.2.1, hence $M, w \models A$.

- A is an instance of (+). This means

$$A \equiv (u : B \lor v : B) \to u + v : B \ .$$

Let

$$M = \langle U, W, H, \mu, * \rangle \in \mathsf{PPJ}_{\mathsf{CS},\mathsf{Meas}}$$

and let $w \in U$ be such that $M, w \models T$. Our goal is to show that $M, w \models A$. The following statements are equivalent:

$$M, w \models A$$
$$\big(M, w \models u : B \text{ or } M, w \models v : B\big) \implies M, w \models (u + v) : B$$
$$\big(B \in u_w^* \text{ or } B \in v_w^*\big) \implies B \in (u + v)_w^* \ .$$

4.2. STRONG COMPLETENESS FOR PJ

The last statement is true according to Definition 2.2.1, hence
$$M, w \models A .$$

- A is an instance of (AN!). This means:
$$A = !^n c : !^{n-1} c : \cdots : !c : c : B$$
where $(c, A) \in \mathsf{CS}$ and $n \in \mathbb{N}$. Let
$$M = \langle U, W, H, \mu, * \rangle \in \mathsf{PPJ}_{\mathsf{CS},\mathsf{Meas}}$$
and let $w \in U$ be such that $M, w \models T$. Our goal is to show that $M, w \models A$. We know that $*_w$ is a CS-evaluation, thus according to Definition 2.2.1 we get:
$$!^{n-1} c : \cdots : !c : c : B \in (!^n c)_w^*$$
i.e.
$$*_w \models !^n c : !^{n-1} c : \cdots : !c : c : B$$
Thus $M, w \models A$.

- A is obtained by an application of (CE). That means $A \equiv P_{\geq 1} B$ and also $\vdash_{\mathsf{PPJ}_{\mathsf{cs}}} B$. Let
$$M = \langle U, W, H, \mu, * \rangle \in \mathsf{PPJ}_{\mathsf{CS},\mathsf{Meas}}$$
and let $w \in U$ be such that $M, w \models T$. Our goal is to show that $M, w \models A$. By i.h. we have that $\emptyset \models B$, i.e. $(\forall M')(\forall x)[M', x \models B]$. In particular we have that for all $x \in U$, $M, x \models B$. So
$$[B]_{M,w} = \{x \in W(w) \mid M, x \models B\} = W(w) ,$$
since $W(w) \subseteq U$. Thus $\mu(w)([B]_{M,w}) = 1$, i.e. $M, w \models P_{\geq 1} B$, i.e.
$$M, w \models A . \qquad \square$$

4.2 Strong Completeness for PJ

In this section constant specifications are always assumed to be constant specifications for the logic J.

In this section we present a strong completeness theorem for the logic PJ, which is obtained by the standard Henkin procedure, i.e. by a canonical model construction. As we mentioned in the introduction, our logic would not be strongly complete without the infinitary rule (ST), since the probabilistic language lacks compactness.

As a first step, we define the notion of consistent sets.

Definition 4.2.1 (L-Consistent Sets). Let L be a logic over the language $\mathcal{L}$ and let $T \subseteq \mathcal{L}$:

- T is L-*consistent* iff $T \nvdash_{\mathsf{L}} \bot$. Otherwise T is said to be L-*inconsistent*.
- T is $\mathcal{L}$-*maximal* iff for every $A \in \mathcal{L}$ either $A \in T$ or $\neg A \in T$.
- T is *maximal* L-*consistent* iff it is $\mathcal{L}$-maximal and L-consistent.

Equivalently we can say that T is L-consistent iff there exists some $A \in \mathcal{L}$ such that $T \nvdash_{\mathsf{L}} A$.

Before proving completeness for PJ we need to prove some auxiliary lemmata and theorems.

Lemma 4.2.2 (Properties of $\mathsf{PJ_{CS}}$-Consistent Sets). *Let* CS *be any constant specification for the logic* J *and let* T *be a* $\mathsf{PJ_{CS}}$-*consistent set.*

(1) For any formula $A \in \mathcal{L}_{\mathsf{PJ}}$ at least one of the sets T, A and $T, \neg A$ is $\mathsf{PJ_{CS}}$-consistent.

(2) If $\neg(A \to P_{\geq s}\beta) \in T$ for $s > 0$, then there is some integer $n \geq \frac{1}{s}$ such that $T, \neg(A \to P_{\geq s - \frac{1}{n}}\beta)$ is $\mathsf{PJ_{CS}}$-consistent.

Proof. (1) Assume that T, A and $T, \neg A$ are both $\mathsf{PJ_{CS}}$-inconsistent, i.e. that $T, A \vdash_{\mathsf{PJ_{CS}}} \bot$ and $T, \neg A \vdash_{\mathsf{PJ_{CS}}} \bot$. Then by **P.R.** and Theorem 3.2.1 we get $T \vdash_{\mathsf{PJ_{CS}}} \bot$, which contradicts the fact that T is $\mathsf{PJ_{CS}}$-consistent. Hence at least one of the sets T, A and $T, \neg A$ is $\mathsf{PJ_{CS}}$-consistent.

(2) Assume that for every integer $n \geq \frac{1}{s}$ the set $T, \neg(A \to P_{\geq s - \frac{1}{n}}\beta)$ is $\mathsf{PJ_{CS}}$-inconsistent. Then we have the following:

$$T, \neg(A \to P_{\geq s - \frac{1}{n}}\beta) \vdash_{\mathsf{PJ_{CS}}} \bot, \qquad \forall n \geq \frac{1}{s} \tag{4.2}$$

$$T \vdash_{\mathsf{PJ_{CS}}} \neg(A \to P_{\geq s - \frac{1}{n}}\beta) \to \bot, \qquad \forall n \geq \frac{1}{s} \quad [\text{Thm. 3.2.1}, (4.2)] \tag{4.3}$$

$$T \vdash_{\mathsf{PJ_{CS}}} A \to P_{\geq s - \frac{1}{n}}\beta, \qquad \forall n \geq \frac{1}{s} \quad [(4.3), \mathbf{P.R.}] \tag{4.4}$$

$$T \vdash_{\mathsf{PJ_{CS}}} A \to P_{\geq s}\beta \qquad\qquad [(4.4), (\mathsf{ST})] \tag{4.5}$$

$$T \vdash_{\mathsf{PJ_{CS}}} \neg(A \to P_{\geq s}\beta) \tag{4.6}$$

$$T \vdash_{\mathsf{PJ_{CS}}} \bot . \qquad\qquad [(4.5), (4.6), \mathbf{P.R.}] \tag{4.7}$$

4.2. STRONG COMPLETENESS FOR PJ   43

Statement (4.7) contradicts the fact that T is $\mathsf{PJ_{CS}}$-consistent. Thus there exists some $n \geq \frac{1}{s}$ such that $T, \neg(A \to P_{\geq s-\frac{1}{n}}\beta)$ is $\mathsf{PJ_{CS}}$-consistent. $\square$

Lemma 4.2.3 establishes some properties of maximal consistent sets. Items (1)–(5) are standard, whereas item (6) is special for our system.

Lemma 4.2.3 (Properties of Maximal $\mathsf{PJ_{CS}}$-Consistent Sets). *Let CS be any constant specification for the logic J and let $\mathcal{T}$ be a maximal $\mathsf{PJ_{CS}}$-consistent set. Then the following hold:*

(1) For any formula $A \in \mathcal{L}_{\mathsf{PJ}}$, exactly one member of $\{A, \neg A\}$ is in $\mathcal{T}$.

(2) For any formula $A \in \mathcal{L}_{\mathsf{PJ}}$:
$$\mathcal{T} \vdash_{\mathsf{PJ_{CS}}} A \Longleftrightarrow A \in \mathcal{T} \ .$$

(3) For all formulas $A, B \in \mathcal{L}_{\mathsf{PPJ}}$ we have:
$$A \vee B \in \mathcal{T} \Longleftrightarrow A \in \mathcal{T} \text{ or } B \in \mathcal{T} \ .$$

(4) For all formulas $A, B \in \mathcal{L}_{\mathsf{PJ}}$ we have:
$$A \wedge B \in \mathcal{T} \Longleftrightarrow \{A, B\} \subseteq \mathcal{T} \ .$$

(5) For all formulas $A, B \in \mathcal{L}_{\mathsf{PJ}}$ we have:
$$\{A, A \to B\} \subseteq \mathcal{T} \Longrightarrow B \in \mathcal{T} \ .$$

(6) Let $\alpha \in \mathcal{L}_\mathsf{J}$, let $X = \{s \mid P_{\geq s}\alpha \in \mathcal{T}\}$ and let $t = \sup(X)$. Then:

  (i) For all $r \in \mathsf{S}[0,t)$ we have that $P_{>r}\alpha \in \mathcal{T}$;

  (ii) For all $r \in \mathsf{S}[0,t)$ we have that $P_{\geq r}\alpha \in \mathcal{T}$;

  (iii) If $t \in \mathsf{S}$ then $P_{\geq t}\alpha \in \mathcal{T}$;

  (iv) For any $r \in \mathsf{S}$:
$$t \geq r \Longleftrightarrow P_{\geq r}\alpha \in \mathcal{T} \ .$$

Proof. (1) By Definition 4.2.1, we know that at least one member of $\{A, \neg A\}$ belongs to $\mathcal{T}$. If both members of $\{A, \neg A\}$ belong to $\mathcal{T}$ then we can easily conclude that $\mathcal{T} \vdash_{\mathsf{PJ_{CS}}} \bot$, which contradicts the fact that $\mathcal{T}$ is $\mathsf{PJ_{CS}}$-consistent. Thus, exactly one member of $\{A, \neg A\}$ belongs to $\mathcal{T}$.

(2) The direction ($\Longleftarrow$) is obvious. We prove the direction ($\Longrightarrow$) by contraposition. Assume that $A \notin \mathcal{T}$. By (1) we have that $\neg A \in \mathcal{T}$. So, by the consistency of $\mathcal{T}$, we cannot have $\mathcal{T} \vdash_{\mathsf{PJ_{cs}}} A$. Thus we have $\mathcal{T} \nvdash_{\mathsf{PJ_{cs}}} A$.

(3) ($\Longleftarrow$) : Assume that $A \in \mathcal{T}$. We have:

$$\mathcal{T} \vdash A \tag{4.8}$$
$$\mathcal{T} \vdash A \vee B . \qquad [(4.8), \mathbf{P.R.}]$$

By the last statement and by (2) we have $A \vee B \in \mathcal{T}$. If $B \in \mathcal{T}$ we prove the claim similarly.

($\Longrightarrow$) : Assume that $A \vee B \in \mathcal{T}$ and that both A and B do not belong in $\mathcal{T}$. By (1) we have that $\{\neg A, \neg B\} \subseteq \mathcal{T}$. Hence we have:

$$\mathcal{T} \vdash \neg A \tag{4.9}$$
$$\mathcal{T} \vdash \neg B \tag{4.10}$$
$$\mathcal{T} \vdash \neg (A \vee B) \qquad [(4.9), (4.10), \mathbf{P.R.}]$$
$$\mathcal{T} \vdash A \vee B .$$

The last two statements contradict the fact that $\mathcal{T}$ is $\mathsf{PJ_{cs}}$-consistent. Thus, at least one of A, B belong to $\mathcal{T}$.

(4) ($\Longleftarrow$) : We have:

$$\mathcal{T} \vdash_{\mathsf{PJ_{cs}}} A \tag{4.11}$$
$$\mathcal{T} \vdash_{\mathsf{PJ_{cs}}} B \tag{4.12}$$
$$\mathcal{T} \vdash_{\mathsf{PJ_{cs}}} A \wedge B \qquad [(4.11), (4.12), \mathbf{P.R.}]$$

By the last statement and by (2) we have $A \wedge B \in \mathcal{T}$.

($\Longrightarrow$) : We have that $\mathcal{T} \vdash_{\mathsf{PJ_{cs}}} A \wedge B$. By **P.R.** we get that $\mathcal{T} \vdash_{\mathsf{PJ_{cs}}} A$ and $\mathcal{T} \vdash_{\mathsf{PJ_{cs}}} B$. By (2) we have that $A, B \in \mathcal{T}$.

(5) We have:

$$\mathcal{T} \vdash_{\mathsf{PJ_{cs}}} A \tag{4.13}$$
$$\mathcal{T} \vdash_{\mathsf{PJ_{cs}}} A \to B \tag{4.14}$$
$$\mathcal{T} \vdash_{\mathsf{PJ_{cs}}} B \qquad [(4.13), (4.14), (\mathbf{MP})] \tag{4.15}$$
$$B \in \mathcal{T} . \qquad [(4.15), (2)]$$

(6) We have:

4.2. STRONG COMPLETENESS FOR PJ

(i) Let $r \in S[0,t)$. Assume that $P_{>r}\alpha \notin \mathcal{T}$. Then assume that for some $r' \in S(r,1]$ we have $P_{\geq r'}\alpha \in \mathcal{T}$. Since $r' > r$ by Lemma 3.2.2(iii) we have that $\mathcal{T} \vdash_{\mathsf{PJ_{CS}}} P_{\geq r'}\alpha \to P_{>r}\alpha$. By (2) we have $P_{\geq r'}\alpha \to P_{>r}\alpha \in \mathcal{T}$ and by (5) we have $P_{>r}\alpha \in \mathcal{T}$ which is absurd since we assumed that $P_{>r}\alpha \notin \mathcal{T}$. Thus, for all $r' \in S(r,1]$ we have $P_{\geq r'}\alpha \notin \mathcal{T}$. Thus r is an upper bound of X, which is again absurd since $r < t$ and $t = \sup(X)$. Hence we conclude that $P_{>r}\alpha \in \mathcal{T}$.

(ii) Let $r \in S[0,t)$. By (i) we have that $P_{>r}\alpha \in \mathcal{T}$. By Lemma 3.2.2(iv) and the maximal consistency of $\mathcal{T}$ we have $P_{>r}\alpha \to P_{\geq r}\alpha \in \mathcal{T}$ and by (5) we get $P_{\geq r}\alpha \in \mathcal{T}$.

(iii) If $t = 0$ then by (P1) we have that $\mathcal{T} \vdash_{\mathsf{PJ_{CS}}} P_{\geq 0}\alpha$. Thus by (2) we have that $P_{\geq t}\alpha \in \mathcal{T}$.
Let $t > 0$. By (ii) we have that for all $n \geq \frac{1}{t}$, $P_{\geq t - \frac{1}{n}}\alpha \in \mathcal{T}$. So by the rule (ST) and the maximal consistency of $\mathcal{T}$ we get $P_{\geq t}\alpha \in \mathcal{T}$.

(iv) Let $r \in S$.
Assume that $P_{\geq r}\alpha \in \mathcal{T}$. Then obviously $t = \sup_s\{P_{\geq s}\alpha \in \mathcal{T}\} \geq r$.
Assume that $t \geq r$. If $t = r$ then by (iii) we get $P_{\geq r}A \in \mathcal{T}$. If $t > r$ then by (ii) we get $P_{\geq r}A \in \mathcal{T}$. □

Now we can prove the well known Lindenbaum Lemma for the logic PJ.

Lemma 4.2.4 (Lindenbaum). *Let CS be any constant specification for the logic J and let T be a $\mathsf{PJ_{CS}}$-consistent set. Then there exists a maximal $\mathsf{PJ_{CS}}$-consistent set $\mathcal{T}$, such that $T \subseteq \mathcal{T}$.*

Proof. Let T be a $\mathsf{PJ_{CS}}$-consistent set. Let $A_0, A_1, A_2, \ldots$ be an enumeration of all the formulas in $\mathcal{L}_{\mathsf{PJ}}$. We define a sequence of sets $\{T_i\}_{i \in \mathbb{N}}$ such that:

(1) $T_0 := T$;

(2) for every $i \geq 0$:

  (a) if $T_i \cup \{A_i\}$ is $\mathsf{PJ_{CS}}$-consistent, then we set $T_{i+1} := T_i \cup \{A_i\}$, otherwise

  (b) if A_i is of the form $B \to P_{\geq s}\gamma$, for $s > 0$, then we choose some integer $n \geq \frac{1}{s}$ such that $T_i \cup \{\neg A_i, \neg(B \to P_{\geq s - \frac{1}{n}}\gamma)\}$ is $\mathsf{PJ_{CS}}$-consistent[1] and we set $T_{i+1} := T_i \cup \{\neg A_i, \neg(B \to P_{\geq s - \frac{1}{n}}\gamma)\}$, otherwise

  (c) we set $T_{i+1} := T_i \cup \{\neg A_i\}$;

---
[1] We will show in the case (ii) below that such an n always exists.

(3) $\mathcal{T} = \bigcup_{i=0}^{\infty} T_i$.

By induction on i we will prove that T_i is PJ$_{\text{CS}}$-consistent for every $i \in \mathbb{N}$.

(i) The consistency of T_0 follows from that of T.

(ii) Let $i \geq 0$. Assuming that T_i is PJ$_{\text{CS}}$-consistent, we will prove that T_{i+1} is PJ$_{\text{CS}}$-consistent. We have the following cases:

- If T_{i+1} is constructed using the case (2)(a) above, then it is obviously PJ$_{\text{CS}}$-consistent.
- If T_{i+1} is constructed using the case (2)(b) above then we know that T_i, A_i is PJ$_{\text{CS}}$-inconsistent, thus according to Lemma 4.2.2(1) we have that $T_i, \neg A_i$ is PJ$_{\text{CS}}$-consistent. We also have that $A_i = B \to P_{\geq s}\gamma$ for $s > 0$. So, according to Lemma 4.2.2(2) we know that there exists some $n \geq \frac{1}{s}$ such that $T_i, \neg A_i, \neg(B \to P_{\geq s-\frac{1}{n}}\gamma)$ is PJ$_{\text{CS}}$-consistent, thus T_{i+1} is PJ$_{\text{CS}}$-consistent.
- If T_{i+1} is constructed using the case (2)(c) above then we know that T_i, A_i is PJ$_{\text{CS}}$-inconsistent, thus according to Lemma 4.2.2(1) we have that $T_i, \neg A_i$ is PJ$_{\text{CS}}$-consistent, i.e. T_{i+1} is PJ$_{\text{CS}}$-consistent.

Now we will show that $\mathcal{T}$ is a maximal PJ$_{\text{CS}}$-consistent set.

We have that for every $A \in \mathcal{L}_{\text{PJ}}$ either $A \in \mathcal{T}$ or $\neg A \in \mathcal{T}$. Thus according to Definition 4.2.1, the set $\mathcal{T}$ is $\mathcal{L}_{\text{PJ}}$-maximal.

It remains to show that $\mathcal{T}$ is PJ$_{\text{CS}}$-consistent. We will first show that $\mathcal{T}$ does not contain all $\mathcal{L}_{\text{PJ}}$-formulas (see (A) below) and then that $\mathcal{T}$ is PJ$_{\text{CS}}$-deductively closed for $\mathcal{L}_{\text{PJ}}$ (see (B) below). The fact that $\mathcal{T}$ is PJ$_{\text{CS}}$-consistent follows easily from (A) and (B).

(A) Assume that for some $A \in \mathcal{L}_{\text{PJ}}$ both A and $\neg A$ belong to $\mathcal{T}$. That means there are i, j such that $A \in T_i$ and $\neg A \in T_j$. Since

$$T_0 \subseteq T_1 \subseteq T_2 \subseteq \ldots,$$

we have that $\{A, \neg A\} \subseteq T_{\max(i,j)}$, which implies that the set $T_{\max(i,j)}$ is PJ$_{\text{CS}}$-inconsistent, a contradiction. Thus, $\mathcal{T}$ does not contain all members of $\mathcal{L}_{\text{PJ}}$.

(B) We show that $\mathcal{T}$ is PJ$_{\text{CS}}$-deductively closed for $\mathcal{L}_{\text{PJ}}$-formulas.

Assume that for some $A \in \mathcal{L}_{\text{PJ}}$ we have that $\mathcal{T} \vdash_{\text{PJ}_{\text{cs}}} A$. We will prove by transfinite induction on the depth of the derivation $\mathcal{T} \vdash_{\text{PJ}_{\text{cs}}} A$ that $A \in \mathcal{T}$. We distinguish cases depending on the last rule or axiom used to obtain A from $\mathcal{T}$.

4.2. STRONG COMPLETENESS FOR PJ

(1) If $A \in \mathcal{T}$ then we are done.

(2) Assume that A is an instance of some PJ-axiom. We know that there exists some k such that $A = A_k$. Assume that $\neg A_k \in T_{k+1}$. Then we have that $T_{k+1} \vdash_{\mathsf{PJ_{CS}}} \neg A_k$ and $T_{k+1} \vdash_{\mathsf{PJ_{CS}}} A_k$ (since A_k is an axiom), which contradicts the fact that T_{k+1} is $\mathsf{PJ_{CS}}$-consistent. Hence, $A_k \in T_{k+1}$, i.e. $A \in \mathcal{T}$.

(3) If A is obtained from $\mathcal{T}$ by an application of the rule (MP), then by the inductive hypothesis we have that all the premises of the rule are contained in $\mathcal{T}$. So there must exist some l such that T_l contains all the premises of the rule. So, $T_l \vdash_{\mathsf{PJ_{CS}}} A$. There exists also some k such that $A = A_k$. Assume that $\neg A \in T_{\max(k,l)+1}$. This implies that $T_{\max(k,l)+1} \vdash_{\mathsf{PJ_{CS}}} A$ and $T_{\max(k,l)+1} \vdash_{\mathsf{PJ_{CS}}} \neg A$, which contradicts the fact that $T_{\max(k,l)+1}$ is $\mathsf{PJ_{CS}}$-consistent. Thus we have that $A \in T_{\max(k,l)+1}$, i.e. $A \in \mathcal{T}$.

(4) Assume that A is obtained by $\mathcal{T}$ by an application of the rule (CE). This means that $A = P_{\geq 1}\alpha$ and that $\vdash_{\mathsf{J_{CS}}} \alpha$ for some $\alpha \in \mathcal{L}_{\mathsf{J}}$. We know that there exists some k such that $A = A_k$. Using the same arguments with case (2) we can prove that $A \in T_{k+1}$, i.e. $A \in \mathcal{T}$.

(5) Assume that A is obtained from $\mathcal{T}$ by the rule (ST). That means that $A = B \to P_{\geq s}\gamma$ for $s > 0$ and also that for every integer $k \geq \frac{1}{s}$ we have $\mathcal{T} \vdash_{\mathsf{PJ_{CS}}} B \to P_{\geq s-\frac{1}{k}}\gamma$. Assume that A does not belong to $\mathcal{T}$, thus $\neg A \in \mathcal{T}$, i.e. $\neg(B \to P_{\geq s}\gamma) \in \mathcal{T}$. Let m be such that $A_m = B \to P_{\geq s}\gamma$. We find that $\neg(B \to P_{\geq s}\gamma) \in T_{m+1}$ and by the construction of $\mathcal{T}$, there exists some $l \geq \frac{1}{s}$ such that $\neg(B \to P_{\geq s-\frac{1}{l}}\gamma) \in T_{m+1}$. However, we also find that the formula $B \to P_{\geq s-\frac{1}{l}}$ is a premise of (ST), thus by the inductive hypothesis $B \to P_{\geq s-\frac{1}{l}} \in \mathcal{T}$. So, there exists an m' such that $B \to P_{\geq s-\frac{1}{l}} \in T_{m'}$. Thus

$$\{\neg(B \to P_{\geq s-\frac{1}{l}}), B \to P_{\geq s-\frac{1}{l}}\} \subseteq T_{\max(m+1,m')},$$

which contradicts the fact that $T_{\max(m+1,m')}$ is $\mathsf{PJ_{CS}}$-consistent. Thus $A \in \mathcal{T}$.

Now we can prove that $\mathcal{T}$ is $\mathsf{PJ_{CS}}$-consistent.

Assume that $\mathcal{T}$ is not $\mathsf{PJ_{CS}}$-consistent. Then we have the following:

$$\mathcal{T} \vdash_{\mathsf{PJ_{CS}}} \bot \tag{4.16}$$

$$(\forall A \in \mathcal{L}_{\mathsf{PJ}})\big[\mathcal{T} \vdash_{\mathsf{PJ_{CS}}} \bot \to A\big] \qquad [(\mathsf{P})] \tag{4.17}$$

$$(\forall A \in \mathcal{L}_{\mathsf{PJ}})\big[\mathcal{T} \vdash_{\mathsf{PJ_{CS}}} A\big] \qquad [(4.16), (4.17), (\mathsf{MP})] \tag{4.18}$$

48 CHAPTER 4. SOUNDNESS AND COMPLETENESS

$$(\forall A \in \mathcal{L}_{\mathsf{PJ}})\bigl[A \in \mathcal{T}\bigr] \, . \qquad [(4.18), (B)] \qquad (4.19)$$

Statement (4.19) contradicts (A), thus $\mathcal{T}$ is $\mathsf{PJ}_{\mathsf{CS}}$-consistent.

So, we proved that $\mathcal{T}$ is a maximal $\mathsf{PJ}_{\mathsf{CS}}$-consistent set that contains the $\mathsf{PJ}_{\mathsf{CS}}$-consistent set T. □

Remark 4.2.5. Since in the logic PJ the proofs may have infinite depth, the usual method for proving the Lindenbaum lemma (i.e. the one used for finitary logics) cannot be applied here. In finitary systems the consistency of the set $\mathcal{T}$ (in the proof of Lemma 4.2.4) is obtained by the consistency of the sets T_i. Since $\mathcal{T} = \cup_{i \in \mathbb{N}} T_i$ the consistency of $\mathcal{T}$, in a finitary system, would simply follow by contradiction:

Assume that $\mathcal{T} \vdash \bot$. Then there should exist some finite $T' \subseteq \mathcal{T}$ such that $T' \vdash \bot$. But then $T' \subseteq T_i$ for some i, which contradicts the consistency of T_i.

However, such an argument cannot be used for an infinitary system. Therefore, we have to change the construction of the sets T_i (in the way we did in Lemma 4.2.4) in order to obtain consistency for $\mathcal{T}$.

Now we will define a canonical model for any maximal $\mathsf{PJ}_{\mathsf{CS}}$-consistent set of formulas.

Definition 4.2.6 (Canonical Model for PJ). Let CS be any constant specification for the logic J and let $\mathcal{T}$ be a maximal $\mathsf{PJ}_{\mathsf{CS}}$-consistent set of $\mathcal{L}_{\mathsf{PJ}}$-formulas. The *canonical model* for $\mathcal{T}$ is the quadruple $M_{\mathcal{T}} = \langle W, H, \mu, * \rangle$, defined as follows:

- $W = \bigl\{ w \mid w \text{ is a CS-evaluation} \bigr\}$;
- $H = \bigl\{ [\alpha]_{M_{\mathcal{T}}} \mid \alpha \in \mathcal{L}_{\mathsf{J}} \bigr\}$;
- for every $\alpha \in \mathcal{L}_{\mathsf{J}}$, $\mu\bigl([\alpha]_{M_{\mathcal{T}}}\bigr) = \sup_s \bigl\{ P_{\geq s}\alpha \in \mathcal{T} \bigr\}$;
- for every $w \in W$, $*_w = w$.

Remark 4.2.7. In Definition 4.2.6 the canonical model $M_{\mathcal{T}} = \langle W, H, \mu, * \rangle$ is defined. Observe that in the definition of H we use the set $[\alpha]_{M_{\mathcal{T}}}$. This is not a problem since by Definition 3.1.6 we have that $[\alpha]_{M_{\mathcal{T}}}$ depends only on $*$, W, and the justification formula α, which do not depend on H. The same holds for μ. Thus, the canonical model is well-defined.

Now we establish the most difficult part of the completeness proof, which is to show that the canonical model is a measurable model.

4.2. STRONG COMPLETENESS FOR PJ

Lemma 4.2.8. *Let* CS *be any constant specification for the logic* J *and let* $\mathcal{T}$ *be a maximal* PJ$_{CS}$*-consistent set. The canonical model for* $\mathcal{T}$, $M_{\mathcal{T}}$, *is a* PJ$_{CS,\text{Meas}}$*-model.*

Proof. Let $M_{\mathcal{T}} = \langle W, H, \mu, * \rangle$. Observe that according to Definition 4.2.6, for every $\alpha \in \mathcal{L}_J$ we have:
$$[\alpha]_{M_{\mathcal{T}}} = \{w \in W \mid *_w \models \alpha\} = \{w \mid w \text{ is a CS-evaluation and } w \models \alpha\} .$$

In order for $M_{\mathcal{T}}$ to be a PJ$_{CS,\text{Meas}}$-model we have to prove the following:

(1) **W is a non-empty set:**

We know that there exists a CS-evaluation, thus $W \neq \emptyset$.

(2) **H is an algebra over W:**

It holds that $[\top] = W$. Thus $W \in H$. Hence $H \neq \emptyset$. Let $[\alpha] \in H$. It holds that $[\alpha] \subseteq W$. Thus $H \subseteq \mathcal{P}(W)$.

Let $\alpha, \beta \in \mathcal{L}_J$ and assume that $[\alpha], [\beta] \in H$. We have that $\neg \alpha, \alpha \vee \beta \in \mathcal{L}_J$ and by Remark 3.1.8 $[\alpha] \cup [\beta] = [\alpha \vee \beta] \in H$ and $W \setminus [\alpha] = [\neg \alpha] \in H$.

So, according to Definition 3.1.1, H is an algebra over W.

(3) **μ is a function from H to $[0,1]$:**

We have to prove the following:

(a) **the domain of μ is H and the codomain of μ is $[0,1]$:**

Let $[\alpha] \in H$ for some $\alpha \in \mathcal{L}_J$. We have that $P_{\geq 0}\alpha$ is an axiom of PJ, thus $P_{\geq 0}\alpha \in \mathcal{T}$. Hence, the set $\{s \in S \mid P_{\geq s}\alpha \in \mathcal{T}\}$ is not empty, which means that it has a supremum. We have that $\mu([\alpha]) = \sup_s\{P_{\geq s}\alpha \in \mathcal{T}\}$. Thus, μ is defined for all members of H, i.e. the domain of μ is H. In $\sup_s\{P_{\geq s}\alpha \in \mathcal{T}\}$ we have by definition that $s \in S$, i.e. $s \leq 1$. By a previous argument it also holds that $\sup_s\{P_{\geq s}\alpha \in \mathcal{T}\} \geq 0$. Thus $0 \leq \sup_s\{P_{\geq s}\alpha \in \mathcal{T}\} \leq 1$, i.e. $0 \leq \mu([\alpha]) \leq 1$. So the codomain of μ is $[0,1]$.

(b) **for every $U \in H$, $\mu(U)$ is unique:**

Let $U \in H$ and assume that $U = [\alpha] = [\beta]$ for some $\alpha, \beta \in \mathcal{L}_J$. We will prove that $\mu([\alpha]) = \mu([\beta])$. Of course it suffices to prove that:

$$[\alpha] \subseteq [\beta] \Longrightarrow \mu([\alpha]) \leq \mu([\beta]) . \tag{4.20}$$

50 CHAPTER 4. SOUNDNESS AND COMPLETENESS

We have:

$$[\alpha] \subseteq [\beta] \qquad \text{implies}$$
$$(\forall w \in W)\big[w \in [\alpha] \implies w \in [\beta]\big] \qquad \text{implies}$$
$$(\forall w \in W)\big[w \models \alpha \implies w \models \beta\big] \qquad \text{implies}$$
$$(\forall w \in W)\big[w \models \alpha \to \beta\big] \qquad \text{implies}$$
$$\models_{\mathsf{CS}} \alpha \to \beta \qquad \text{implies by}$$
$$\text{Theorem 2.3.3}$$
$$\vdash_{\mathsf{J_{CS}}} \alpha \to \beta \qquad \text{implies by}$$
$$\text{Lemma 3.2.2(ii)}$$
$$(\forall s \in \mathsf{S})\big[\vdash_{\mathsf{PJ_{CS}}} P_{\geq s}\alpha \to P_{\geq s}\beta\big] \qquad \text{implies by}$$
$$\text{Lemma 4.2.3(2)}$$
$$(\forall s \in \mathsf{S})\big[P_{\geq s}\alpha \to P_{\geq s}\beta \in \mathcal{T}\big] \qquad \text{implies by}$$
$$\text{Lemma 4.2.3(5)}$$
$$(\forall s \in \mathsf{S})\big[P_{\geq s}\alpha \in \mathcal{T} \implies P_{\geq s}\beta \in \mathcal{T}\big] \qquad \text{implies}$$
$$\{s \in \mathsf{S} \mid P_{\geq s}\alpha \in \mathcal{T}\} \subseteq \{s \in \mathsf{S} \mid P_{\geq s}\beta \in \mathcal{T}\} \qquad \text{implies}$$
$$\sup_s\{P_{\geq s}\alpha \in \mathcal{T}\} \leq \sup_s\{P_{\geq s}\beta \in \mathcal{T}\} \qquad \text{i.e.}$$
$$\mu([\alpha]) \leq \mu([\beta]) \ .$$

Hence (4.20) holds, which proves that $\mu(U)$ is unique.

(4) μ is a finitely additive measure:

Before proving that μ is a finitely additive measure we need to prove the following statement:

$$\mu([\alpha]) + \mu([\neg\alpha]) \leq 1 \ . \tag{4.21}$$

Let:

$$X = \{s \mid P_{\geq s}\alpha \in \mathcal{T}\} \ ;$$
$$Y = \{s \mid P_{\geq s}\neg\alpha \in \mathcal{T}\} \ ;$$
$$r_1 = \mu([\alpha]) = \sup(X) \ ;$$
$$r_2 = \mu([\neg\alpha]) = \sup(Y) \ .$$

Let $s \in Y$. It holds that $P_{\geq s}\neg\alpha \in \mathcal{T}$. If $1 - s < r_1$ then by Lemma 4.2.3(6)(i) we would have $P_{>1-s}\alpha \in \mathcal{T}$. By **S.E.** we get $\neg P_{\leq 1-s}\alpha \in \mathcal{T}$ and by **S.E.** again we get $\neg P_{\geq s}\neg\alpha \in \mathcal{T}$ which contradicts the fact that $\mathcal{T}$ is $\mathsf{PJ_{CS}}$-consistent.

4.2. STRONG COMPLETENESS FOR PJ

Thus $1 - s \geq r_1$, i.e. $1 - r_1 \geq s$, i.e. $1 - r_1$ is an upper bound of Y, hence $1 - r_1 \geq r_2$, i.e. $r_1 + r_2 \leq 1$, i.e. (4.21) holds.

Now in order to prove that μ is a finitely additive measure we need to prove the following:

(i) $\boldsymbol{\mu(W) = 1}$.
  We have that $\vdash_{\mathsf{J_{CS}}} \top$. By the rule (CE) we get $\vdash_{\mathsf{PJ_{CS}}} P_{\geq 1}\top$. By Lemma 4.2.3(2) we get $P_{\geq 1}\top \in \mathcal{T}$. It holds that $W = [\top]$. Thus $\mu(W) = \mu([\top]) = \sup_s\{P_{\geq s}\top \in \mathcal{T}\} \geq 1$, i.e. $\mu(W) = 1$.

(ii) $[\alpha] \cap [\beta] = \emptyset \Longrightarrow \boldsymbol{\mu([\alpha] \cup [\beta]) = \mu([\alpha]) + \mu([\beta])}$.
  Let $\alpha, \beta \in \mathcal{L}_\mathsf{J}$ such that:

$$[\alpha] \cap [\beta] = \emptyset\ ;$$
$$r = \mu([\alpha]) = \sup_s\left\{s \mid P_{\geq s}\alpha \in \mathcal{T}\right\}\ ;$$
$$s = \mu([\beta]) = \sup_r\left\{r \mid P_{\geq r}\ ; \beta \in \mathcal{T}\right\}\ ;$$
$$t_0 = \mu([\alpha \vee \beta]) = \sup_t\{P_{\geq t}(\alpha \vee \beta) \in \mathcal{T}\}\ .$$

Our aim is to show that:
$$t_0 = r + s\ .$$

It holds $[\beta] \subseteq [\neg\alpha]$. By (4.20) we have $\mu([\beta]) \leq \mu([\neg\alpha])$ and by (4.21) we have:

$$\mu([\beta]) \leq 1 - \mu([\alpha])$$
$$\text{i.e. } s \leq 1 - r$$
$$\text{i.e. } r + s \leq 1\ . \tag{4.22}$$

We also have that

$$\mu([\neg(\alpha \wedge \beta)]) = \mu(W \setminus ([\alpha] \cap [\beta])) = \mu(W) = 1\ .$$

Thus $1 = \sup_s\{P_{\geq s}\neg(\alpha \wedge \beta) \in \mathcal{T}\}$. So, by Lemma 4.2.3(6)(iii) we find

$$P_{\geq 1}\neg(\alpha \wedge \beta) \in \mathcal{T}\ . \tag{4.23}$$

We distinguish the following cases:

- Suppose that $r > 0$ and $s > 0$. By Lemma 4.2.3(6)(ii) we have that for every $r' \in \mathsf{S}[0, r)$ and every $s' \in \mathsf{S}[0, s)$, $P_{\geq r'}\alpha$, $P_{\geq s'}\beta \in \mathcal{T}$. It holds that $r' + s' < r + s$ and by (4.22) we get $r' + s' < 1$. Thus by (4.23) and by axiom (**DIS**) we get $P_{\geq r'+s'}(\alpha \vee \beta) \in \mathcal{T}$. Hence $t_0 = \sup_t\{P_{\geq t}(\alpha \vee \beta) \in \mathcal{T}\} \geq r+s$.

If $r+s = 1$ then we have that $t_0 = 1$, i.e. $t_0 = r+s$.

If $r+s < 1$ then since $r, s > 0$ we have that $r, s < 1$. Assume that $r+s < t_0$. By Lemma 4.2.3(6)(ii) for every $t' \in S(r+s, t_0)$ we have $P_{\geq t'}(\alpha \vee \beta) \in \mathcal{T}$. We choose rational numbers r'' and s'' such that $t' = r'' + s''$ and $r'' > r$ and $s'' > s$. If we had $P_{\geq r''}\alpha, P_{\geq s''}\beta \in \mathcal{T}$ this would imply that

$$\mu([\alpha]) = \sup_s\{s \mid P_{\geq s}\alpha \in \mathcal{T}\} = r \geq r''$$

and

$$\mu([\beta]) = \sup_r\{r \mid P_{\geq r}\beta \in \mathcal{T}\} = s \geq s'',$$

which is absurd since $r'' > r$ and $s'' > s$. Thus we have:

$$\neg P_{\geq r''}\alpha \in \mathcal{T}, \neg P_{\geq s''}\beta \in \mathcal{T}$$

and by **S.E.** we get:

$$P_{<r''}\alpha \in \mathcal{T}, P_{<s''}\beta \in \mathcal{T}.$$

By Axiom (**LE**) we get:

$$P_{\leq r''}\alpha \in \mathcal{T}, P_{<s''}\beta \in \mathcal{T}.$$

It holds that $r'' + s'' = t' < t_0 \leq 1$. Thus by Axiom (**UN**) we get: $P_{<r''+s''}(\alpha \vee \beta) \in \mathcal{T}$ and by **S.E.** $\neg P_{\geq r''+s''}(\alpha \vee \beta) \in \mathcal{T}$, i.e.
$$\neg P_{\geq t'}(\alpha \vee \beta) \in \mathcal{T},$$
which is a contradiction since $P_{\geq t'}(\alpha \vee \beta) \in \mathcal{T}$ and $\mathcal{T}$ is PJ$_{\text{CS}}$-consistent. Thus $r + s = t_0$.

- Assume that at least one of r, s is equal to 0. Then we can reason as in the above case with the only exception that $r' = 0$ or $s' = 0$ (depending on whether $r = 0$ or $s = 0$ respectively).

(5) **for all $w \in W$, $*_w$ is a CS-evaluation.**

It holds by the construction of $M_\mathcal{T}$.

(6) **for all $\alpha \in \mathcal{L}_J$, $[\alpha]_{M_\mathcal{T}} \in H$.**

It holds by the construction of $M_\mathcal{T}$. □

Now we prove that the model for a maximal consistent set $\mathcal{T}$ satisfies all the formulas in $\mathcal{T}$.

4.2. STRONG COMPLETENESS FOR PJ

Lemma 4.2.9 (Truth Lemma for PJ). *Let* CS *be a constant specification. Let* $\mathcal{T}$ *be a maximal* PJ$_{CS}$-*consistent set of* $\mathcal{L}_{PJ}$-*formulas and let* $M_\mathcal{T}$ *be the canonical model for* $\mathcal{T}$*. We have:*

$$(\forall A \in \mathcal{L}_{PJ})[A \in \mathcal{T} \iff M_\mathcal{T} \models A] \ .$$

Proof. We prove the claim by induction on the structure of $A \in \mathcal{L}_{PJ}$. We distinguish the following cases:

$\boldsymbol{A \equiv P_{\geq s}\alpha}$: The following statements are equivalent:

$$\begin{aligned}
& M_\mathcal{T} \models A \\
& M_\mathcal{T} \models P_{\geq s}\alpha \\
& \mu([\alpha]_{M_\mathcal{T}}) \geq s \\
& \sup_r \left\{ P_{\geq r}\alpha \in \mathcal{T} \right\} \geq s && \text{[Definition 4.2.6]} \\
& P_{\geq s}\alpha \in \mathcal{T} && \text{[Lemma 4.2.3(6)}(iv)\text{]} \\
& A \in \mathcal{T} \ .
\end{aligned}$$

$\boldsymbol{A \equiv \neg B}$: The following statements are equivalent:

$$\begin{aligned}
& A \in \mathcal{T} \\
& \neg B \in \mathcal{T} \\
& B \notin \mathcal{T} && \text{[Lemma 4.2.3(1)]} \\
& M_T \not\models B && \text{[i.h.]} \\
& M_T \not\models \neg A \\
& M_T \models A \ .
\end{aligned}$$

$\boldsymbol{A \equiv B \wedge C}$: The following statements are equivalent:

$$\begin{aligned}
& A \in \mathcal{T} \\
& B \wedge C \in \mathcal{T} \\
& B \in \mathcal{T} \text{ and } C \in \mathcal{T} && \text{[Lemma 4.2.3(4)]} \\
& M_T \models B \text{ and } M_T \models C && \text{[i.h.]} \\
& M_T \models B \wedge C \\
& M_T \models A \ . && \square
\end{aligned}$$

And finally we can establish strong completeness for PJ.

Theorem 4.2.10 (Strong Completeness for PJ). *Let* CS *be any constant specification for the logic* J, *let* $T \subseteq \mathcal{L}_{PJ}$ *and let* $A \in \mathcal{L}_{PJ}$. *Then we have:*

$$T \models_{\mathsf{PJ}_{\mathsf{CS},\mathsf{Meas}}} A \iff T \vdash_{\mathsf{PJ}_{\mathsf{CS}}} A \ .$$

Proof. The direction $\Longleftarrow$ follows from Theorem 4.1.2.
We prove the direction $\Longrightarrow$ by contraposition. Assume that $T \nvdash_{\mathsf{PJ}_{\mathsf{CS}}} A$. This means that $T \nvdash_{\mathsf{PJ}_{\mathsf{CS}}} (\neg A) \to \bot$. By Theorem 3.2.1 we get $T, \neg A \nvdash_{\mathsf{PJ}_{\mathsf{CS}}} \bot$, i.e. the set $T, \neg A$ is $\mathsf{PJ}_{\mathsf{CS}}$-cosistent. By Lemma 4.2.4 there exists a maximal $\mathsf{PJ}_{\mathsf{CS}}$-consistent set $\mathcal{T}$ such that $\mathcal{T} \supseteq T \cup \{\neg A\}$. By Lemma 4.2.9 we have that $M_{\mathcal{T}} \models T$ and $M_{\mathcal{T}} \models \neg A$. By Lemma 4.2.8 we have that $M_{\mathcal{T}} \in \mathsf{PJ}_{\mathsf{CS},\mathsf{Meas}}$. Hence $T \nvDash_{\mathsf{PJ}_{\mathsf{CS},\mathsf{Meas}}} A$. □

4.3 Strong Completeness for PPJ

In this section constant specifications are always assumed to be constant specifications for the logic PPJ.

The strong completeness theorem for the logic PPJ is obtained by a canonical model construction. Most of the lemmata and theorems needed for the proof are proved very similarly to the ones for the logic PJ. However, in order to deal with iterated probabilities and with justifications over probabilities we need to employ some ideas from the completeness proof for the probabilistic logic LPP_1 [ORM09] and from the completeness proof for the justification logic J [Art12, KS12].

It is straightforward to show that Remark 3.1.8 and Lemmata 3.1.13, 3.2.2, 4.2.2, 4.2.3 and 4.2.4 also hold for the logic PPJ. So, in order to complete the completeness proof we have to define the canonical model for $\mathsf{PPJ}_{\mathsf{CS}}$ and show that it is a measurable $\mathsf{PPJ}_{\mathsf{CS}}$-model.

Definition 4.3.1 (Canonical Model for PPJ). *Let* CS *be a constant specification for the logic* PPJ. *The canonical model for* $\mathsf{PPJ}_{\mathsf{CS}}$ *is the quintuple*

$$M = \langle U, W, H, \mu, * \rangle \ ,$$

defined as follows:

- $U = \left\{ w \mid w \text{ is a maximal } \mathsf{PPJ}_{\mathsf{CS}}\text{-consistent set of } \mathcal{L}_{\mathsf{PPJ}}\text{-formulas} \right\}$;

- for every $w \in U$ the probability space $\langle W(w), H(w), \mu(w) \rangle$ is defined as follows:

4.3. STRONG COMPLETENESS FOR PPJ

   (i) $W(w) = U$;

   (ii) $H(w) = \{(A)_M \mid A \in \mathcal{L}_{\mathsf{PPJ}}\}$ where $(A)_M = \{x \mid x \in U, A \in x\}$; [2]

   (iii) for all $A \in \mathcal{L}_{\mathsf{PPJ}}$, $\mu(w)\big((A)_M\big) = \sup_s \{P_{\geq s}A \in w\}$;

- for every $w \in W$ the CS-evaluation $*_w$ is defined as follows:

   1. for all $p \in \mathsf{Prop}$:
   $$p_w^* = \begin{cases} \mathsf{T} & \text{, if } p \in w\,; \\ \mathsf{F} & \text{, if } \neg p \in w\,; \end{cases}$$

   2. for all $t \in \mathsf{Tm}$:
   $$t_w^* = \{A \mid t : A \in w\}\,.$$

We now prove some properties of the set $(A)_M$.

Lemma 4.3.2. *Let $M = \langle U, W, H, \mu, * \rangle$ be the canonical model for some $\mathsf{PPJ}_{\mathsf{CS}}$ and let $A, B \in \mathcal{L}_{\mathsf{PPJ}}$. Then the following hold:*

(i) $(\neg A)_M = U \setminus (A)_M$;

(ii) $(A)_M \cap (B)_M = (A \wedge B)_M$;

(iii) $(A)_M \cup (B)_M = (A \vee B)_M$.

Proof. (i) We have:
$$\begin{aligned}(\neg A) &= \{x \mid x \in U, \neg A \in x\} \\ &\stackrel{\text{Lemma 4.2.3(1)}}{=} \{x \mid x \in U, A \notin x\} \\ &= U \setminus (A)\,.\end{aligned}$$

(ii) We have:
$$\begin{aligned}(A) \cap (B) &= \{x \mid x \in U, A \in x\} \cap \{x \mid x \in U, B \in x\} \\ &= \{x \mid x \in U, A \in x \text{ and } B \in x\} \\ &\stackrel{\text{Lemma 4.2.3(4)}}{=} \{x \mid x \in U, A \wedge B \in x\} \\ &= (A \wedge B)\,.\end{aligned}$$

---

[2] If M is clear from the context, we may simply write (A) instead of $(A)_M$.

(iii) We have:

$$(A) \cup (B) = \{x \mid x \in U, A \in x\} \cup \{x \mid x \in U, B \in x\}$$
$$= \{x \mid x \in U, A \in x \text{ or } B \in x\}$$
$$\stackrel{\text{Lemma 4.2.3(3)}}{=} \{x \mid x \in U, A \vee B \in x\}$$
$$= (A \vee B) \ . \qquad \square$$

Now we will prove that the canonical model for PPJ$_{CS}$ is a PPJ$_{CS}$-model.

Lemma 4.3.3. *Let* CS *be a constant specification for* PPJ. *The canonical model for* PPJ$_{CS}$ *is a* PPJ$_{CS}$-*model*.

Proof. Let $M = \langle U, W, H, \mu, * \rangle$ be the canonical model for PPJ$_{CS}$. In order for M to be a PPJ$_{CS}$-model we have to prove the following:

U is a non-empty set:

There exists a PPJ$_{CS}$-maximal consistent set. Thus $U \neq \emptyset$.

For every $w \in U$ the triple $\langle W(w), H(w), \mu(w) \rangle$ is a probability space:

We have to prove the following:

(1) **$W(w)$ is a non-empty subset of U:**

It is obvious since $W(w) = U$ and $U \neq \emptyset$.

(2) **$H(w)$ is an algebra over $W(w)$:**

It holds that:

$$(\top)_M = \{x \mid x \in U, \top \in x\} = U = W(w) \ .$$

Thus $W(w) \in H(w)$.

Let $(A)_M \in H(w)$ for some $A \in \mathcal{L}_{\mathsf{PPJ}}$. It holds that:

$$(A)_M = \{x \mid x \in U, A \in x\} \subseteq U = W(w) \ .$$

Thus $H(w) \subseteq \mathcal{P}(W(w))$.

Let $(A), (B) \in H(w)$ for some $A, B \in \mathcal{L}_{\mathsf{PPJ}}$. By Lemma 4.3.2 we have that $W(w) \setminus (A) = U \setminus (A) = (\neg A) \in H(w)$ and that $(A) \cup (B) = (A \vee B) \in H(w)$. So, according to Definition 3.1.1, $H(w)$ is an algebra over $W(w)$.

(3) **$\mu(w)$ is a function from $H(w)$ to $[0, 1]$:**

We have to prove the following:

4.3. STRONG COMPLETENESS FOR PPJ

(a) **The domain of $\mu(w)$ is $H(w)$ and the codomain of $\mu(w)$ is $[0,1]$:**

Let $(A) \in H(w)$. We have that $P_{\geq 0}A$ is an axiom of PPJ, thus $P_{\geq 0}A \in w$. Hence the set $\{s \in S \mid P_{\geq s}A \in w\}$ is not empty which means that it has a supremum. So $\mu(w)((A))$ is defined. Thus the domain of $\mu(w)$ is $H(w)$.

Let $(A) \in H(w)$. By a previous argument we have that
$$\mu(w)((A)) = \sup_s \{P_{\geq s}A \in w\} \geq 0 \ .$$

In $\sup_s\{P_{\geq s}A \in w\}$ we have by definition that $s \in \mathsf{S}$, i.e. $s \leq 1$. Thus $\sup_s\{P_{\geq s}A \in w\} \leq 1$, i.e. $\mu(w)\big((A)\big) \leq 1$. So the codomain of $\mu(w)$ is $[0,1]$.

(b) **For every $V \in H(w)$, $\mu(w)(V)$ is unique:**

Let $V \in H(w)$ and assume that $V = (A) = (B)$ for some $A, B \in \mathcal{L}_{\mathsf{PPJ}}$. We will prove that $\mu(w)\big((A)\big) = \mu(w)\big((B)\big)$. Of course, it suffices to prove that:
$$(A) \subseteq (B) \implies \mu(w)\big((A)\big) \leq \mu(w)\big((B)\big) \ . \tag{4.24}$$

We have:

$$\begin{aligned}
(A) \subseteq (B) & \qquad \text{implies} \\
(\forall x \in U)\big[x \in (A) \implies x \in (B)\big] & \qquad \text{implies} \\
(\forall x \in U)\big[A \in x \implies B \in x\big] & \qquad \text{implies} \\
(\forall x \in U)\big[A \notin x \text{ or } B \in x\big] & \qquad \text{implies by} \\
& \qquad \text{Lemma 4.2.3(1)} \\
(\forall x \in U)\big[\neg A \in x \text{ or } B \in x\big] & \qquad \text{implies by} \\
& \qquad \text{Lemma 4.2.3(3)} \\
(\forall x \in U)\big[\neg A \vee B \in x\big] & \qquad \text{implies by S.E.} \\
(\forall x)\big[x \text{ is a maximal } \mathsf{PPJ_{CS}}\text{-consistent set} & \qquad (4.25) \\
\implies A \to B \in x\big] \ . &
\end{aligned}$$

Assume that $\not\vdash A \to B$. By **P.R.** we get $\not\vdash \neg(A \to B) \to \bot$. By Theorem 3.2.1 we get $\neg(A \to B) \not\vdash \bot$, which implies that the set $\{\neg(A \to B)\}$ is $\mathsf{PPJ_{CS}}$-consistent. By Lemma 4.2.4 we have that there exists a maximal $\mathsf{PPJ_{CS}}$-cosistent set $\mathcal{T}$ such that
$$\mathcal{T} \supseteq \{\neg(A \to B)\} \ .$$

58   CHAPTER 4. SOUNDNESS AND COMPLETENESS

However by statement (4.25) we have that $A \to B \in \mathcal{T}$ which contradicts the fact that $\mathcal{T}$ is $\mathsf{PPJ_{CS}}$-consistent. Thus $\vdash A \to B$. Therefore, by Lemma 3.2.2(ii) we have that $(\forall s \in \mathsf{S}) \big[\vdash P_{\geq s}A \to P_{\geq s}B \big]$. Hence, since w is a maximal $\mathsf{PPJ_{CS}}$-consistent set, we get the following:

$(\forall s \in \mathsf{S})\big[P_{\geq s}A \to P_{\geq s}B \in w\big]$ implies by L. 4.2.3(5)

$(\forall s \in \mathsf{S})\big[P_{\geq s}A \in w \Longrightarrow P_{\geq s}B \in w\big]$ implies

$\{s \in \mathsf{S} \mid P_{\geq s}A \in w\} \subseteq \{s \in \mathsf{S} \mid P_{\geq s}B \in w\}$ implies

$\sup_s\{P_{\geq s}A \in w\} \leq \sup_s\{P_{\geq s}B \in w\}$ i.e.

$\mu(w)\big((A)\big) \leq \mu(w)\big((B)\big)$.

Hence statement (4.24) holds, which proves that $\mu(w)(V)$ is unique.

(4) $\mu(w)$ is a finitely additive measure:

The proof for this claim is identical to the proof for the analogue claim in Theorem 4.2.10 that is why it is omitted.

For every $w \in W$, $*_w$ is a CS-evaluation:

According to Definition 4.3.1, $*_w$ maps every atomic proposition to a truth value and every term to a set of $\mathcal{L}_{\mathsf{PPJ}}$-formulas. Now we need to show that $*_w$ satisfies the properties of a CS-evaluation according to Definition 2.2.1.

Let $A, B \in \mathcal{L}_{\mathsf{PPJ}}$, let $c \in \mathsf{Con}$ and let $u, v \in \mathsf{Tm}$. We need to show that:

(a) $\big(A \to B \in u_w^* \text{ and } A \in v_w^*\big) \Longrightarrow B \in (u \cdot v)_w^*$:

Let $A \in v_w^*$ and let $A \to B \in u_w^*$. By Definition 4.3.1 we have that $u : (A \to B) \in w$ and that $v : A \in w$. By axiom (J), by (MP) and by the fact that w is a maximal $\mathsf{PPJ_{CS}}$-consistent set we get that $u \cdot v : B \in w$. By Definition 4.3.1 we have that $B \in (u \cdot v)_w^*$.

(b) $u_w^* \cup v_w^* \subseteq (u + v)_w^*$:

Let $B \in u_w^* \cup v_w^*$. Assume that $B \in u_w^*$. This means that $u : B \in w$. By (+) and (MP) we get that $u + v : B \in w$, i.e. $B \in (u + v)_w^*$. If $B \in v_w^*$ then we proceed similarly.

(c) For $(c, A) \in \mathsf{CS}$ and for all $n \in \mathbb{N}$ we have that:

$$!^{n-1}c :!^{n-2}c : \cdots :!c : c : A \in (!^n c)_w^* \ .$$

4.3. STRONG COMPLETENESS FOR PPJ

Assume that $(c, A) \in \text{CS}$. Then by rule (AN!) we get that for all $n \in \mathbb{N}$:

$$\vdash_{\text{PPJ}_{\text{CS}}} !^n c :!^{n-1} c : \cdots :!c : c : A \ .$$

By Lemma 4.2.3(2) we have that for all $n \in \mathbb{N}$:

$$!^n c :!^{n-1} c : \cdots :!c : c : A \in w \ .$$

By Definition 4.3.1 we have that for all $n \in \mathbb{N}$:

$$!^{n-1} c :!^{n-2} c : \cdots :!c : c : A \in (!^n c)_w^* \ . \qquad \square$$

Before proving that the canonical model is a $\text{PPJ}_{\text{CS,Meas}}$-model we need the following auxiliary lemma.

Lemma 4.3.4. *Let $M = \langle U, W, H, \mu, * \rangle$ be the canonical model for some PPJ_{CS}. Then we have:*

$$(\forall A \in \mathcal{L}_{\text{PPJ}})(\forall w \in U)\big[[A]_{M,w} = (A)_M\big].$$

Proof. Let $w \in U$ and let $A \in \mathcal{L}_{\text{PPJ}}$. We will prove the claim by induction on the structure of A. We distinguish the following cases:

1. $A \equiv p \in \text{Prop}$. It holds that:

$$[A]_{M,w} = [p]_{M,w} = \{x \in W(w) \mid M, x \models p\} = \{x \in U \mid p_x^* = \mathsf{T}\}$$
$$= \{x \in U \mid p \in x\} = (p)_M = (A)_M \ .$$

2. $A \equiv t : B$. It holds that:

$$[A]_{M,w} = [t : B]_{M,w} = \{x \in W(w) \mid M, x \models t : B\} = \{x \in U \mid B \in t_x^*\}$$
$$= \{x \in U \mid t : B \in x\} = (t : B)_M = (A)_M \ .$$

3. $A \equiv P_{\geq s} B$. By the inductive hypothesis we have that for all $x \in U$,

$$[B]_{M,x} = (B)_M \ .$$

And of course it holds that $[B]_{M,x} \in H(x)$, since $(B)_M \in H(x)$. Thus, we have:

$$\begin{aligned}
[A]_{M,w} = [P_{\geq s} B]_{M,w} &= \{x \in W(w) \mid M, x \models P_{\geq s} B\} \\
&= \{x \in W(w) \mid \mu(x)\big([B]_{M,x}\big) \geq s\} \\
&= \{x \in W(w) \mid \mu(x)\big((B)_M\big) \geq s\} \\
&= \{x \in U \mid \sup_r \{P_{\geq r} B \in x\} \geq s\} \ .
\end{aligned}$$

By Lemma 4.2.3(6)(iv) we get:

$$[P_{\geq s} B]_{M,w} = \{x \in U \mid P_{\geq s} B \in x\} = (P_{\geq s} B)_M = (A)_M \ .$$

4. $A \equiv B \wedge C$. It holds that:

$$[A]_{M,w} = [B \wedge C]_{M,w} = [B]_{M,w} \cap [C]_{M,w} \stackrel{\text{i.h.}}{=} (B)_{M,w} \cap (C)_{M,w}$$
$$\stackrel{\text{Lemma 4.3.2}(ii)}{=} (B \wedge C)_{M,w} = (A)_M .$$

5. $A \equiv \neg B$. It holds that:

$$[A]_{M,w} = [\neg B]_{M,w} = W(w) \setminus [B]_{M,w} \stackrel{\text{i.h.}}{=} U \setminus (B)_{M,w}$$
$$\stackrel{\text{Lemma 4.3.2}(i)}{=} (\neg B)_{M,w} = (A)_M .$$

□

From Lemma 4.3.4 we get the following corollary.

Corollary 4.3.5. *The canonical model for any* PPJ$_{\text{CS}}$ *is a* PPJ$_{\text{CS,Meas}}$*-model.*

Proof. Let $M = \langle U, W, H, \mu, * \rangle$ be the canonical model for some PPJ$_{\text{CS}}$ and let $A \in \mathcal{L}_{\text{PPJ}}$. For any $w \in U$, by Lemma 4.3.4, we have that $[A]_{M,w} = (A)_M \in H(w)$. Thus, $M \in$ PPJ$_{\text{CS,Meas}}$. □

Making use of the properties of maximal consistent sets, we can establish the Truth Lemma for the logic PPJ.

Lemma 4.3.6 (Truth Lemma for PPJ). *Let* CS *be some constant specification for the logic* PPJ *and let* $M = \langle U, W, H, \mu, * \rangle$ *be the canonical model for* PPJ$_{\text{CS}}$. *For every* $A \in \mathcal{L}_{\text{PPJ}}$ *and any* $w \in U$ *we have:*

$$A \in w \iff M, w \models A .$$

Proof. We prove the claim by induction on the structure of A. We distinguish the following cases:

$A = p \in$ Prop. It holds:

$$M, w \models A \iff$$
$$M, w \models p \iff$$
$$p_w^* = \mathsf{T} \stackrel{\text{Definition 4.3.1}}{\iff}$$
$$p \in w \iff$$
$$A \in w .$$

4.3. STRONG COMPLETENESS FOR PPJ

$A = t : B$. It holds:

$$\begin{aligned}
M, w \models A & \iff \\
M, w \models t : B & \iff \\
B \in t_w^* & \overset{\text{Definition 4.3.1}}{\iff} \\
t : B \in w & \iff \\
A \in w\,. &
\end{aligned}$$

$A = P_{\geq s} B$. It holds:

$$\begin{aligned}
M, w \models A & \iff \\
M, w \models P_{\geq s} B & \iff \\
\mu(w)\big([B]_{M,w}\big) \geq s & \overset{\text{Lemma 4.3.4}}{\iff} \\
\mu(w)\big((B)_M\big) \geq s & \overset{\text{Definition 4.3.1}}{\iff} \\
\sup_r \{P_{\geq r} B \in w\} \geq s & \overset{\text{Lemma 4.2.3(6)}(iv)}{\iff} \\
P_{\geq s} B \in w & \iff \\
A \in w\,. &
\end{aligned}$$

$A = \neg B$: It holds:

$$\begin{aligned}
M, w \models A & \iff \\
M, w \models \neg B & \iff \\
M, w \not\models B & \overset{\text{i.h.}}{\iff} \\
B \notin w & \overset{\text{Lemma 4.2.3(1)}}{\iff} \\
\neg B \in w & \iff \\
A \in w\,. &
\end{aligned}$$

$A = B \wedge C$: It holds:

$$\begin{aligned}
M, w \models A & \iff \\
M, w \models B \wedge C & \iff \\
M, w \models B \text{ and } M, w \models C & \overset{\text{i.h.}}{\iff} \\
B \in w \text{ and } C \in w & \overset{\text{Lemma 4.2.3(4)}}{\iff} \\
B \wedge C \in w & \iff \\
A \in w\,. &
\end{aligned}$$ □

Finally, we get the strong completeness theorem for the logic PPJ.

Theorem 4.3.7 (Strong Completeness for PPJ). *Let $T \subseteq \mathcal{L}_{\mathsf{PPJ}}$ and let $A \in \mathcal{L}_{\mathsf{PPJ}}$. Then, for any $\mathsf{PPJ}_{\mathsf{CS}}$ we have:*

$$T \vdash_{\mathsf{PPJ}_{\mathsf{CS}}} A \iff T \models_{\mathsf{PPJ}_{\mathsf{CS},\mathsf{Meas}}} A .$$

Proof. We prove the two directions of the equivalence separately:

$\Longrightarrow$: It follows from Theorem 4.1.3.

$\Longleftarrow$: Let CS be any constant specification for the logic PPJ. We prove the claim by contraposition. Assume that $T \nvdash_{\mathsf{PPJ}_{\mathsf{CS}}} A$. This means that $T \nvdash_{\mathsf{PPJ}_{\mathsf{CS}}} (\neg A) \to \bot$. By Theorem 3.3.9 we get $T, \neg A \nvdash_{\mathsf{PPJ}_{\mathsf{CS}}} \bot$, i.e. the set $T \cup \{\neg A\}$ is $\mathsf{PPJ}_{\mathsf{CS}}$-cosistent. By Lemma 4.2.4 there exists a maximal $\mathsf{PPJ}_{\mathsf{CS}}$-consistent set of formulas w such that $w \supseteq T \cup \{\neg A\}$. Let M be the canonical model for $\mathsf{PPJ}_{\mathsf{CS}}$. By Corollary 4.3.5 we have that $M \in \mathsf{PPJ}_{\mathsf{CS},\mathsf{Meas}}$. By Lemma 4.3.6 we have that $M, w \models T$ and $M, w \models \neg A$. Hence $T \nvDash_{\mathsf{PPJ}_{\mathsf{CS},\mathsf{Meas}}} A$. □

Chapter 5
Decidability and Complexity

In this chapter we present decidability procedures for the probabilistic justification logics PJ and PPJ. Our algorithms are combinations of decidability algorithms for the logic J [Kuz00, Kuz08] and decidability algorithms for probabilistic logics [FHM90, ORM09]. Note that in the case of PPJ these combinations are not trivial, due to the presence of formulas of the form $t : P_{\geq s} A$. Our decidability procedures make use of well known results from the theory of linear programming. In the case of PJ we also establish upper and lower complexity bounds.

The results for this chapter are drawn from [Kok16, KOS16].

5.1 Small Model Property for PJ

The goal of this section is to prove a small model property for the logic PJ. The small model property will be the most important tool for establishing the upper bound for the complexity of the satisfiability problem in the logic PJ.

In this section constant specifications are always assumed to be constant specifications for the logic J.

Definition 5.1.1 (Subformulas). The set $\mathsf{subf}(\cdot)$ is defined recursively as follows: For $\mathcal{L}_J$-formulas:

- $\mathsf{subf}(p) := \{p\}$;
- $\mathsf{subf}(t : \alpha) := \{t : \alpha\} \cup \mathsf{subf}(\alpha)$;
- $\mathsf{subf}(\neg \alpha) := \{\neg \alpha\} \cup \mathsf{subf}(\alpha)$;
- $\mathsf{subf}(\alpha \wedge \beta) := \{\alpha \wedge \beta\} \cup \mathsf{subf}(\alpha) \cup \mathsf{subf}(\beta)$.

CHAPTER 5. DECIDABILITY AND COMPLEXITY

For $\mathcal{L}_{\mathsf{PJ}}$-formulas:

- $\mathsf{subf}(P_{\geq s}\alpha) := \{P_{\geq s}\alpha\} \cup \mathsf{subf}(\alpha)$;
- $\mathsf{subf}(\neg A) := \{\neg A\} \cup \mathsf{subf}(A)$;
- $\mathsf{subf}(A \wedge B) := \{A \wedge B\} \cup \mathsf{subf}(A) \cup \mathsf{subf}(B)$.

Observe that for $A \in \mathcal{L}_{\mathsf{PJ}}$ we have that $\mathsf{subf}(A) \subseteq \mathcal{L}_{\mathsf{PJ}} \cup \mathcal{L}_{\mathsf{J}}$.

Definition 5.1.2 (Atoms). Let A be an $\mathcal{L}_{\mathsf{PJ}}$- or an $\mathcal{L}_{\mathsf{J}}$-formula. Let X be the set that contains all the atomic propositions and the justification assertions from the set $\mathsf{subf}(A)$. An atom of A is any formula of the following form:

$$\bigwedge_{B \in X} \pm B ,$$

where $\pm B$ denotes either B or $\neg B$. We will use the lowercase Latin letter a for atoms, possibly with subscripts.

Let A that of the form $\bigwedge_i B_i$ or of the form $\bigvee_i B_i$. Then $C \in A$ means that for some i, $B_i = C$.

Definition 5.1.3 (Sizes). The size function $|\cdot|$ is defined as follows:
For $\mathcal{L}_{\mathsf{PJ}}$-formulas: (recursively)

- $|P_{\geq s}\alpha| := 2$;
- $|\neg A| := 1 + |A|$;
- $|A \wedge B| := |A| + 1 + |B|$.

For sets:
Let W be a set. $|W|$ is the cardinal number of W.
For non-negative integers:
Let r be an non-negative integer. We define the size of r to be equal to the length of r written in binary, i.e.:

$$|r| := \begin{cases} 1 & , r = 0 ; \\ \lfloor \log_2(r) \rfloor + 1 & , r \geq 1 , \end{cases}$$

where $\lfloor \cdot \rfloor$ is the function that returns the greatest integer that is less than or equal to its argument.
For non-negative rational numbers:
Let $r = \frac{s_1}{s_2}$, where s_1 and s_2 are relatively prime non-negative integers with $s_2 \neq 0$, be a non-negative rational number. We define:

$$|r| := |s_1| + |s_2| .$$

5.1. SMALL MODEL PROPERTY FOR PJ

Let $A \in \mathcal{L}_{\mathsf{PJ}}$ we define:

$$||A|| := \max\left\{|s| \;\Big|\; P_{\geq s}\alpha \in \mathsf{subf}(A)\right\}.$$

A proof for Theorem 5.1.4 can be found in [Chv83, p. 145].

Theorem 5.1.4. *Let $\mathcal{S}$ be a system of r linear equalities. Assume that the vector[1] $\boldsymbol{x}$ is a solution of $\mathcal{S}$ such that all of $\boldsymbol{x}$'s entries are non-negative. Then there is a vector $\boldsymbol{x}^*$ such that:*

(1) $\boldsymbol{x}^*$ is a solution of $\mathcal{S}$;

(2) all the entries of $\boldsymbol{x}^*$ are non-negative;

(3) at most r entries of $\boldsymbol{x}^*$ are positive.

Theorem 5.1.5 establishes some properties for the solutions of a linear system.

Theorem 5.1.5. *Let $\mathcal{S}$ be a linear system of n variables and of r linear equalities and/or inequalities with integer coefficients each of size at most l. Assume that the vector $\boldsymbol{x} = x_1, \ldots, x_n$ is a solution of $\mathcal{S}$ such that for all $i \in \{1, \ldots, n\}$, $x_i \geq 0$. Then there is a vector $\boldsymbol{x}^* = x_1^*, \ldots, x_n^*$ with the following properties:*

(1) $\boldsymbol{x}^*$ is a solution of $\mathcal{S}$;

(2) for all i, x_i^* is a non-negative rational number with size bounded by

$$2 \cdot \Big(r \cdot l + r \cdot \log_2(r) + 1\Big).$$

(3) at most r entries of $\boldsymbol{x}^*$ are positive;

(4) for all $i \in \{1, \ldots, n\}$, if $x_i^* > 0$ then $x_i > 0$;

Proof. In $\mathcal{S}$ we replace the variables that correspond to the entries of $\boldsymbol{x}$ that are equal to zero (if any) with zeros. This way we obtain a new linear system $\mathcal{S}_0$, with r linear equalities and/or inequalities and $m \leq n$ variables. $\boldsymbol{x}$ is a solution[2] of $\mathcal{S}_0$. It also holds that any solution of $\mathcal{S}_0$ is a solution[3] of $\mathcal{S}$.

---

[1]We will always use bold font for vectors.
[2]In the proof of Theorem 5.1.5 all vectors have n entries. The entries of the vectors are assumed to be in one to one correspondence with the variables that appear in the original system $\mathcal{S}$.
 Let $\boldsymbol{y}$ be a solution of a linear system $\mathcal{T}$. If $\boldsymbol{y}$ has more entries than the variables of $\mathcal{T}$ we imply that entries of $\boldsymbol{y}$ that correspond to variables that appear in $\mathcal{T}$ compose a solution of $\mathcal{T}$.
[3]Assume that system $\mathcal{T}$ has less variables than system $\mathcal{T}'$. When we say that any solution of $\mathcal{T}$ is a solution of $\mathcal{T}'$ we imply that the missing variables are set to 0.

Assume that the system $\mathcal{S}_0$ contains an inequality of the form

$$b_1 \cdot y_1 + \ldots + b_m \cdot y_m \lozenge c \tag{5.1}$$

for $\lozenge \in \{<, \leq, \geq, >\}$ where $y_1, \ldots, y_m$ are variables of $\mathcal{S}$ and $b_1, \ldots, b_m, c$ are constants that appear in $\mathcal{S}$. $\boldsymbol{x}$ is a solution of (5.1). We replace the inequality (5.1) in $\mathcal{S}_0$ with the following equality:

$$b_1 \cdot y_1 + \ldots + b_m \cdot y_m = b_1 \cdot x_1 + \ldots + b_m \cdot x_m \; .$$

We repeat this procedure for every inequality of $\mathcal{S}_0$. This way we obtain a system of linear equalities which we call $\mathcal{S}_1$. It is easy to see that $\boldsymbol{x}$ is a solution of $\mathcal{S}_1$ and that any solution of $\mathcal{S}_1$ is also a solution of $\mathcal{S}_0$ and thus of $\mathcal{S}$.

Now we will transform $\mathcal{S}_1$ to another linear system by applying the following algorithm.

Algorithm:
We set $i = 1$, $e_i = r$, $v_i = m$, $\boldsymbol{x}^i = \boldsymbol{x}$ and we execute the following steps:

(i) If $e_i = v_i$ then go to step (ii). Otherwise go to step (iii).

(ii) If the determinant of $\mathcal{S}_i$ is non-zero then stop. Otherwise go to step (v).

(iii) If $e_i < v_i$ then go to step (iv), else go to step (v).

(iv) We know that the vector $\boldsymbol{x}^i$ is a non-negative solution for the system $\mathcal{S}_i$. From Theorem 5.1.4 we obtain a solution $\boldsymbol{x}^{i+1}$ for the system $\mathcal{S}_i$ which has at most e_i entries positive. In $\mathcal{S}_i$ we replace the variables that correspond to zero entries of the solution $\boldsymbol{x}^{i+1}$ with zeros. We obtain a new system which we call $\mathcal{S}_{i+1}$ with e_{i+1} equalities and v_{i+1} variables. $\boldsymbol{x}^{i+1}$ is a solution of $\mathcal{S}_{i+1}$ and any solution of $\mathcal{S}_{i+1}$ is a solution of $\mathcal{S}_i$. We set $i := i + 1$ and we go to step (i).

(v) From any set of equalities that are linearly dependent we keep only one equation. We obtain a new system which we call $\mathcal{S}_{i+1}$ with e_{i+1} equalities and v_{i+1} variables. We set $i := i + 1$ and $\boldsymbol{x}^{i+1} := \boldsymbol{x}^i$. We go to step (i).

Let I be the final value of i after the execution of the algorithm. Since the only way for our algorithm to terminate is through step (ii) it holds that system $\mathcal{S}_I$ is an $e_I \times e_I$ system of linear equalities with non-zero determinant (for $e_I \leq r$). System $\mathcal{S}_I$ is obtained from system $\mathcal{S}_1$ by possibly replacing some variables that correspond to zero entries of the solution with zeros and by possibly removing some linearly dependent equalities. So, any solution of $\mathcal{S}_I$ is also a solution of system

5.1. SMALL MODEL PROPERTY FOR PJ

$\mathcal{S}_1$ and thus a solution of $\mathcal{S}$. From the algorithm we have that $\boldsymbol{x}^I$ is a solution of $\mathcal{S}_I$. Since $\mathcal{S}_I$ has a non-zero determinant Cramer's rule can be applied. Hence, the vector $\boldsymbol{x}^I$ is the unique solution of system $\mathcal{S}_I$. Let x_i^I be an entry of $\boldsymbol{x}^I$. x_i^I will be equal to the following rational number

$$\frac{\begin{vmatrix} a_{11} & \cdots & a_{1e_I} \\ & \ddots & \\ a_{e_I 1} & \cdots & a_{e_I e_I} \end{vmatrix}}{\begin{vmatrix} b_{11} & \cdots & b_{1e_I} \\ & \ddots & \\ b_{e_I 1} & \cdots & b_{e_I e_I} \end{vmatrix}}$$

where all the a_{ij} and b_{ij} are integers that appear in the original system $\mathcal{S}$. By properties of the determinant we know that the numerator and the denominator of the above rational number will each be at most equal to $r! \cdot (2^l - 1)^r$. So we have that:

$$|x_i^I| \leq 2 \cdot \left(\log_2(r! \cdot (2^l - 1)^r) + 1 \right) \quad \Longrightarrow$$
$$|x_i^I| \leq 2 \cdot \left(\log_2(r^r \cdot 2^{l \cdot r}) + 1 \right) \quad \Longrightarrow$$
$$|x_i^I| \leq 2 \cdot \left(r \cdot \log_2(r) + l \cdot r + 1 \right).$$

As we already mentioned the final vector $\boldsymbol{x}^I$ is a solution of the original linear system $\mathcal{S}$. We also have that all the entries of $\boldsymbol{x}^I$ are non-negative, at most r of its entries are positive and the size of each entry of $\boldsymbol{x}^I$ is bounded by $2 \cdot (r \cdot \log_2 r + r \cdot l + 1)$. Furthermore, since the variables that correspond to zero entries of the original vector $\boldsymbol{x}$ were replaced by zeros, we have that for every i, if the i-th entry of $\boldsymbol{x}^I$ is positive then the i-th entry of $\boldsymbol{x}$ is positive too. So, $\boldsymbol{x}^I$ is the requested vector $\boldsymbol{x}^*$. □

Theorem 5.1.6 is an adaptation of the small model theorem from [FHM90]. Similar techniques have also been used in [ORM09] to obtain decidability for the logic LPP$_2$. Observe, that the small model obtained in Theorem 5.1.6 is not only small in terms of possible worlds, it is also small in terms of the probabilities and the CS-evaluations that are assigned to each world. Otherwise decidability for PJ would not follow from the small model property.

Theorem 5.1.6 (Small Model Property for PJ). *Let* CS *be any constant specification for the logic* J *and let* $A \in \mathcal{L}_{\mathsf{PJ}}$. *If* A *is* PJ$_{\mathsf{CS,Meas}}$-*satisfiable then it is satisfiable in a* PJ$_{\mathsf{CS,Meas}}$-*model* $M = \langle W, H, \mu, * \rangle$ *such that:*

(1) $|W| \leq |A|$.

(2) $H = \mathcal{P}(W)$.

(3) For every $w \in W$, $\mu(\{w\})$ is a rational number with size at most

$$2 \cdot \Big(|A| \cdot ||A|| + |A| \cdot \log_2(|A|) + 1\Big).$$

(4) For every $V \in H$

$$\mu(V) = \sum_{w \in V} \mu(\{w\}).$$

(5) For every atom of A, a, there exists at most one $w \in W$ such that $*_w \models a$.

Proof. Let CS be any constant specification for the logic J and let $A \in \mathcal{L}_{\mathsf{PJ}}$. Let $a_1, \ldots, a_n$ be all the atoms of A. By propositional reasoning (in the logic $\mathsf{PJ}_{\mathsf{CS}}$) we can prove that:

$$\mathsf{PJ}_{\mathsf{CS}} \vdash A \leftrightarrow \bigvee_{i=1}^{K} \bigwedge_{j=1}^{l_i} P_{\diamondsuit_{ij} s_{ij}}(\beta^{ij})$$

where all the $P_{\diamondsuit_{ij} s_{ij}}(\beta^{ij})$ appear in A and $\diamondsuit_{ij} \in \{\geq, <\}$.

By using propositional reasoning again (but this time in the logic J_{CS}) we can prove that each β^{ij} is equivalent to a disjunction of some atoms of A. So, by using Lemma 3.2.2(ii) we have that:

$$\mathsf{PJ}_{\mathsf{CS}} \vdash A \leftrightarrow \bigvee_{i=1}^{K} \bigwedge_{j=1}^{l_i} P_{\diamondsuit_{ij} s_{ij}}(\alpha^{ij})$$

where each α^{ij} is a disjunction of some atoms of A. By Theorem 4.2.10 we have that for any $M \in \mathsf{PJ}_{\mathsf{CS},\mathsf{Meas}}$:

$$M \models A \iff M \models \bigvee_{i=1}^{K} \bigwedge_{j=1}^{l_i} P_{\diamondsuit_{ij} s_{ij}}(\alpha^{ij}). \tag{5.2}$$

Assume that A is satisfiable. By Eq. (5.2) there must exist some i such that

$$\bigwedge_{j=1}^{l_i} P_{\diamondsuit_{ij} s_{ij}}(\alpha^{ij})$$

is satisfiable. Let $M' = \langle W', H', \mu', *' \rangle$ be a $\mathsf{PJ}_{\mathsf{CS},\mathsf{Meas}}$-model such that:

$$M' \models \bigwedge_{j=1}^{l_i} P_{\diamondsuit_{ij} s_{ij}}(\alpha^{ij}). \tag{5.3}$$

5.1. SMALL MODEL PROPERTY FOR PJ

For every $k \in \{1, \ldots, n\}$ we define:

$$x_k = \mu'([a_k]_{M'}) . \tag{5.4}$$

In every world of M' some atom of A must hold. Thus, we have:

$$W' = \bigcup_{k=1}^{n} [a_k]_{M'} .$$

And since $\mu'(W') = 1$ we get:

$$\mu'\left(\bigcup_{k=1}^{n} [a_k]_{M'}\right) = 1 . \tag{5.5}$$

The a_k's are atoms of the same formula, so we have:

$$k \neq k' \implies [a_k]_{M'} \cap [a_{k'}]_{M'} = \emptyset . \tag{5.6}$$

By Eqs. (5.5), (5.6) and the fact that μ' is a finitely additive measure we get:

$$\sum_{k=1}^{n} \mu'([a_k]_{M'}) = 1$$

and by Eq. (5.4):

$$\sum_{k=1}^{n} x_k = 1 . \tag{5.7}$$

Let $j \in \{1, \ldots, l_i\}$. From Eq. (5.3) we get:

$$M' \models P_{\Diamond_{ij} s_{ij}}\left(\alpha^{ij}\right).$$

This implies that $\mu'([\alpha^{ij}]_{M'}) \Diamond_{ij} s_{ij}$, i.e.

$$\mu'\left(\left[\bigvee_{a_k \in \alpha^{ij}} a_k\right]_{M'}\right) \Diamond_{ij} s_{ij}$$

which by Remark 3.1.8 implies that

$$\mu'\left(\bigcup_{a_k \in \alpha^{ij}} [a_k]_{M'}\right) \Diamond_{ij} s_{ij} .$$

By Eq. (5.6) and the additivity of μ' we have that:

$$\sum_{a_k \in \alpha^{ij}} \mu'([a_k]_{M'}) \Diamond_{ij} s_{ij}$$

and by Eq. (5.4):
$$\sum_{a_k \in \alpha^{ij}} x_k \lozenge_{ij} s_{ij} .$$

So we have that

$$\text{for every } j \in \{1, \ldots, l_i\}, \sum_{a_k \in \alpha^{ij}} x_k \lozenge_{ij} s_{ij} . \tag{5.8}$$

Let $\mathcal{S}$ be the following linear system:

$$\sum_{k=1}^{n} z_k = 1$$
$$\sum_{a_k \in \alpha^{i1}} z_k \lozenge_{i1} s_{i1}$$
$$\vdots$$
$$\sum_{a_k \in \alpha^{il_i}} z_k \lozenge_{il_i} s_{il_i}$$

where the variables of the system are $z_1, \ldots, z_n$. We have the following:

(i) By Eqs. (5.7) and (5.8) the vector $\boldsymbol{x} = x_1, \ldots, x_n$ is a solution of $\mathcal{S}$.

(ii) By Eq. (5.4) every x_k is non-negative.

(iii) Every s_{ij} is a rational number with size at most $||A||$.

(iv) System $\mathcal{S}$ has at most $|A|$ equalities and inequalities.

From (i)-(iv) and Theorem 5.1.5 we have that there exists a vector

$$\boldsymbol{y} = y_1, \ldots, y_n$$

such that:

(I) $\boldsymbol{y}$ is a solution of $\mathcal{S}$.

(II) Every y_i is a non-negative rational number with size at most

$$2 \cdot \left(|A| \cdot ||A|| + |A| \cdot \log_2(|A|) + 1 \right) .$$

(III) At most $|A|$ entries of $\boldsymbol{y}$ are positive.

(IV) For all i, if $y_i > 0$ then $x_i > 0$.

5.1. SMALL MODEL PROPERTY FOR PJ

Without loss of generality we assume that $y_1, \ldots, y_N$ are the positive entries of $\boldsymbol{y}$, where
$$0 < N \leq |A| \ . \tag{5.9}$$
We define the quadruple $M = \langle W, H, \mu, * \rangle$ as follows:

(a) $W = \{w_1, \ldots, w_N\}$, for some $w_1, \ldots, w_N$.

(b) $H = \mathcal{P}(W)$.

(c) For all $V \in H$:
$$\mu(V) = \sum_{w_k \in V} y_k \ .$$

(d) Let $i \in \{1, \ldots, N\}$. We define $*_{w_i}$ to be some CS-evaluation that satisfies the atom a_i. Since y_i is positive, by (IV), x_i is positive too, i.e. $\mu'([a_i]_{M'}) > 0$, which means that $[a_i]_{M'} \neq \emptyset$, i.e. that the atom a_i is CS-satisfiable.

It holds:
$$\mu(W) = \sum_{w_k \in W} y_k$$
$$= \sum_{k=1}^{n} y_k$$
$$\stackrel{(I)}{=} 1$$

Let $U, V \in H$ such that $U \cap V = \emptyset$. It hods:
$$\mu(U \cup V) = \sum_{w_k \in U \cup V} y_k$$
$$= \sum_{w_k \in U} y_k + \sum_{w_k \in V} y_k$$
$$= \mu(U) + \mu(V) \ .$$

Thus μ is a finitely additive measure. By Definitions 3.1.4 and 3.1.6 we have that $M \in \mathsf{PJ}_{\mathsf{CS,Meas}}$.

We will now prove the following statement:
$$(\forall 1 \leq k \leq n)\Big[w_k \in [\alpha^{ij}]_M \iff a_k \in \alpha^{ij}\Big] \ . \tag{5.10}$$

Let $k \in \{1, \ldots, n\}$. We prove the two directions of Eq. (5.10) separately.

($\Longrightarrow$:) Assume that $w_k \in [\alpha^{ij}]$. This means that $*_{w_k} \models \alpha^{ij}$. Assume that $a_k \notin \alpha^{ij}$. Then, since α^{ij} is a disjunction of some atoms of A, there must exist some $a_{k'} \in \alpha^{ij}$, with $k \neq k'$, such that $*_{w_k} \models a_{k'}$. However, by definition we have that $*_{w_k} \models a_k$. But this is a contradiction, since a_k and $a_{k'}$ are different atoms of the same formula, which means that they cannot be satisfied by the same CS-evaluation. Hence, $a_k \in \alpha^{ij}$.

($\Longleftarrow$:) Assume that $a_k \in \alpha^{ij}$. We know that $*_{w_k} \models a_k$, which implies that

$$*_{w_k} \models \alpha^{ij}, \text{ i.e. } w_k \in [\alpha^{ij}]_M .$$

Hence, Eq. (5.10) holds. Now, we will prove the following statement:

$$\left(\forall 1 \leq j \leq l_i\right)\left[M \models P_{\Diamond_{ij} s_{ij}} \alpha^{ij}\right] . \tag{5.11}$$

Let $j \in \{1, \ldots, l_i\}$. It holds

$$M \models P_{\Diamond_{ij} s_{ij}}(\alpha^{ij}) \qquad \Longleftrightarrow$$
$$\mu([\alpha^{ij}]_M) \Diamond_{ij} s_{ij} \qquad \Longleftrightarrow$$
$$\sum_{w_k \in [\alpha^{ij}]_M} y_k \Diamond_{ij} s_{ij} \qquad \overset{\text{Eq. (5.10)}}{\Longleftrightarrow}$$
$$\sum_{a_k \in \alpha^{ij}} y_k \Diamond_{ij} s_{ij} .$$

The last statement holds because of (I). Thus, Eq. (5.11) holds.

By Eq. (5.11) we have that $M \models \bigwedge_{j=1}^{l_i} P_{\Diamond_{ij} s_{ij}}(\alpha^{ij})$, which implies that

$$M \models \bigvee_{i=1}^{K} \bigwedge_{j=1}^{l_i} P_{\Diamond_{ij} s_{ij}}(\alpha^{ij}),$$

which, by Eq. (5.2), implies that $M \models A$.

Let $w_k \in W$. It holds:

$$\mu(\{w_k\}) = \sum_{w_i \in \{w_k\}} y_i = y_k . \tag{5.12}$$

Now we will show that conditions (1)–(5) in the theorem's statement hold.

- Condition (1) holds because of (a) and Eq. (5.9).
- Condition (2) holds because of (b).
- Condition (3) holds because of Eq. (5.12) and (II).

- For every $V \in H$, because of Eq. (5.12), we have:
$$\mu(V) = \sum_{w_k \in V} y_k = \sum_{w_k \in V} \mu(\{w_k\}) .$$
Hence condition (4) holds.

- By (d) every world of M satisfies a unique atom of α. Thus condition (5) holds.

So, M is the model in question. $\square$

5.2 Complexity Bounds for PJ

In this section constant specifications are always assumed to be constant specifications for the logic J.

Lemma 5.2.1 states that if two CS-evaluations agree on some atom of a justification formula then they agree on the formula itself.

Lemma 5.2.1. *Let* CS *be any constant specification. Let* $\alpha \in \mathcal{L}_J$ *and let* a *be an atom of* α. *Let* $*_1, *_2$ *be two* CS-*evaluations and assume that*
$$*_1 \models a \iff *_2 \models a .$$
Then we have:
$$*_1 \models \alpha \iff *_2 \models \alpha .$$

Proof. We prove the claim by induction on the structure of α.

- Assume that α is an atomic proposition or a justification assertion. Then it must be either $\alpha \in a$ or $\neg \alpha \in a$. Thus, since $*_1$ and $*_2$ agree on a they must also agree on α, i.e. $*_2 \models \alpha \iff *_1 \models \alpha$.

- If the top connective of α is $\neg$ or $\wedge$ then the claim follows easily by the inductive hypothesis. $\square$

Lemma 5.2.2. *Let* $\alpha \in \mathcal{L}_J$ *and let* a *be an atom of* α. *Let* $*$ *be a* CS-*evaluation and assume that* $* \models a$. *The decision problem*

$$\text{does } * \text{ satisfy } \alpha ?$$

belongs to the complexity class P.

Proof. We prove the claim by induction on the structure of α.

- Assume that α is an atomic proposition or a justification assertion. Then it must be either $\alpha \in a$ or $\neg \alpha \in a$. If $\alpha \in a$ then we have $* \models \alpha$ and if $\neg \alpha \in a$ then $* \not\models \alpha$. Obviously this check can be done in polynomial time.

- If the top connective of α is $\neg$ or $\wedge$ then the claim follows easily by the inductive hypothesis. □

Recall that in Section 2.3 we pointed out that Kuznets' algorithm [Kuz00] for the J_CS-satisfiability problem is divided in two parts: the saturation algorithm and the completion algorithm. A complexity evaluation for the completion algorithm (using our notation) is stated in Theorem 5.2.3.

Theorem 5.2.3. *Let* CS *be a decidable and schematic constant specification. Let a be an atom of some $\mathcal{L}_\mathsf{J}$-formula. The decision problem*

is a J_CS-satisfiable?

belongs to the complexity class coNP.

Now we are ready to prove the upper bound for the complexity of the $\mathsf{PJ}_{\mathsf{CS},\mathsf{Meas}}$-satisfiability problem.

Theorem 5.2.4. *Let* CS *be a decidable and schematic constant specification. The $\mathsf{PJ}_{\mathsf{CS},\mathsf{Meas}}$-satisfiability problem belongs to the complexity class* Σ_2^p.

Proof. First we will describe an algorithm that decides the problem in question and we will explain its correctness. Then we will evaluate the complexity of the algorithm.

Algorithm:

Let $A \in \mathcal{L}_\mathsf{PJ}$. It suffices to guess a small $\mathsf{PJ}_{\mathsf{CS},\mathsf{Meas}}$-model $M = \langle W, H, \mu, * \rangle$ that satisfies A and also satisfies the conditions (1)–(5) that appear in the statement of Theorem 5.1.6. We guess M as follows: we guess n atoms of A, call them $a_1, \ldots, a_n$, and we also choose n worlds, $w_1, \ldots, w_n$, for $n \leq |A|$. Applying Theorem 5.2.3 we verify that for each $i \in \{1, \ldots, n\}$ there exists a CS-evaluation $*_i$ such that $*_i \models a_i$. We define $W = \{w_1, \ldots, w_n\}$. For every $i \in \{1, \ldots, n\}$ we set $*_{w_i} = *_i$. Since we are only interested in the satisfiability of justification formulas that appear in A, by Lemma 5.2.1, the choice of the $*_{w_i}$ is not important (as long as $*_{w_i}$ satisfies a_i).

We assign to every $\mu(\{w_i\})$ a rational number with size at most:

$$2 \cdot \left(|A| \cdot ||A|| + |A| \cdot \log_2(|A|) + 1\right).$$

5.2. COMPLEXITY BOUNDS FOR PJ

We set $H = \mathcal{P}(W)$. For every $V \in H$ we set:

$$\mu(V) = \sum_{w_i \in V} \mu(\{w_i\}) \ .$$

It is then straightforward to see that conditions (1)–(5) that appear in the statement of Theorem 5.1.6 hold.

Now we have to verify that our guess is correct, i.e. that $M \models A$. Assume that $P_{\geq s}\alpha$ appears in A. In order to see whether $P_{\geq s}\alpha$ holds we need to calculate the measure of the set $[\alpha]_M$ in the model M. The set $[\alpha]_M$ will contain every $w_i \in W$ such that $*_{w_i} \models \alpha$. Since $*_{w_i}$ satisfies an atom of A it also satisfies an atom of α. So, by Lemma 5.2.2, we can check whether $*_{w_i}$ satisfies α in polynomial time. If $\sum_{w_i \in [\alpha]_M} \mu(\{w_i\}) \geq s$ then we replace $P_{\geq s}\alpha$ in A with the truth value T, otherwise with the truth value F. We repeat the above procedure for every formula of the form $P_{\geq s}\alpha$ that appears in A. At the end we have a formula that is constructed only from the connectives $\neg$, $\wedge$ and the truth constants T and F. Obviously, we can verify in polynomial time that the formula is true. This, of course, implies that $M \models A$.

Complexity Evaluation:
All the objects that are guessed in our algorithm have size that is polynomial on A. Also the verification phase of our algorithm can be made in polynomial time. Furthermore the application of Theorem 5.2.3 is possible with an NP-oracle (an NP-oracle can obviously decide coNP problems too). Thus our algorithm is an $\mathsf{NP}^{\mathsf{NP}}$ algorithm and since $\Sigma_2^p = \mathsf{NP}^{\mathsf{NP}}$ the claim of the theorem follows. □

The lower complexity bound for the $\mathsf{PJ}_{\mathsf{CS,Meas}}$-satisfiability problem can be proved much easier.

Theorem 5.2.5. *Let* CS *be a decidable, schematic and axiomatically appropriate constant specification. The* $\mathsf{PJ}_{\mathsf{CS,Meas}}$-*satisfiability problem is* Σ_2^p-*hard.*

Proof. We can prove that the J_{CS}-satisfiability problem can be reduced to the $\mathsf{PJ}_{\mathsf{CS,Meas}}$-satisfiability problem as follows:
Let $\alpha \in \mathcal{L}_\mathsf{J}$. We will prove that:

$$\alpha \text{ is } \mathsf{J}_{\mathsf{CS}}\text{-satisfiable} \iff P_{\geq 1}\alpha \text{ is } \mathsf{PJ}_{\mathsf{CS,Meas}}\text{-satisfiable}.$$

For the direction $\Longrightarrow$:

Assume that there exists a CS-evalution $*$, such that $* \models \alpha$. Then we can construct the quadruple $M = \langle W, H, \mu, *' \rangle$ with

$$W = \{w\} ;$$
$$H = \{\emptyset, \{w\}\} ;$$
$$\mu(\emptyset) = 0 ;$$
$$\mu(\{w\}) = 1 ;$$
$$*'_w = * .$$

It is then straightforward to show that $M \in \mathsf{PJ_{CS,Meas}}$ and that $M \models P_{\geq 1}\alpha$. Thus $P_{\geq 1}\alpha$ is $\mathsf{PJ_{CS,Meas}}$-satisfiable.

For the direction $\Longleftarrow$:

Assume that there exists a $\mathsf{PJ_{CS,Meas}}$-model $M = \langle W, H, \mu, * \rangle$ such that

$$M \models P_{\geq 1}\alpha, \text{ i.e. } \mu([\alpha]_M) \geq 1.$$

If $[\alpha]_M = \emptyset$ then it should be $\mu([\alpha]_M) = 0$ which contradicts the fact that $\mu([\alpha]_M) \geq 1$. Hence, there is a $w \in W$ such that $*_w \models \alpha$. Thus, α is $\mathsf{J_{CS}}$-satisfiable.

So, we proved that the $\mathsf{J_{CS}}$-satisfiability problem can be reduced to the $\mathsf{PJ_{CS,Meas}}$-satisfiability problem. By Theorem 2.3.5 the $\mathsf{J_{CS}}$-satisfiability problem is Σ_2^p-hard. Hence, the $\mathsf{PJ_{CS,Meas}}$-satisfiability problem is Σ_2^p-hard too. □

From Theorems 4.2.10, 5.2.4 and 5.2.5 we can get the following corollary.

Corollary 5.2.6. *Let CS be any decidable, schematic and axiomatically appropriate constant specification. The $\mathsf{PJ_{CS,Meas}}$-satisfiability problem is Σ_2^p-complete and the $\mathsf{PJ_{CS}}$-derivability problem is Π_2^p-complete.*

Remark 5.2.7. Let CS be any decidable, schematic and axiomatically appropriate constant specification. By Corollary 2.3.6 we have that the $\mathsf{J_{CS}}$-derivability problem belongs to the class Π_2^p-complete. By Corollary 5.2.6 we have that the $\mathsf{PJ_{CS}}$-derivability problem belongs to the class Π_2^p-complete too. So, adding probability operators to the justification logic J does not increase the complexity of the logic, although it makes the language more expressive.

5.3 Decidability for PPJ

In this section constant specifications are always assumed to be constant specifications for the logic PPJ.

5.3. DECIDABILITY FOR PPJ

Assume that we want to test some $A \in \mathcal{L}_{\mathsf{PPJ}}$ for satisfiability. The test is divided in two parts: first we test whether the "justification and classical constraints" that appear in A are satisfiable and then we test whether the "probabilistic constraints" that appear in A are satisfiable. Of course we have to make sure that both kinds of constraints are satisfied in the same $\mathsf{PPJ}_{\mathsf{CS},\mathsf{Meas}}$-model. The satisfiability testing for the "justification and classical constraints" will be done using an adaptation of the satisfiability algorithm for the logic J, whereas the satisfiability testing for the "probabilistic constraints" will be done using similar ideas as the ones used for the satisfiability testing in the logic PJ. In order to formally present our satisfiability algorithm we will first explain what is meant under "satisfiability testing for justification and classical constraints", then what is formally meant under "satisfiability testing for probabilistic constraints" and finally how both kind of constraints can be satisfied at the same model.

By testing satisfiability of "justification and classical constraints" that appear in an $\mathcal{L}_{\mathsf{PPJ}}$-formula we mean that we test whether a CS-evaluation satisfies an $\mathcal{L}_{\mathsf{PPJ}}$-formula. In order to formally define the sentence "a CS-evaluation satisfies an $\mathcal{L}_{\mathsf{PPJ}}$-formula" we have to extend the definition of a CS-evaluation.

Definition 5.3.1 (Extended CS-Evaluation). Let CS be any constant specification. An extended CS-evaluation, is a function $*$ that maps atomic propositions and $\mathcal{L}_{\mathsf{PPJ}}$-formulas of the form $P_{\geq s}A$ to truth values and maps justification terms to sets of $\mathcal{L}_{\mathsf{PPJ}}$-formulas such that the conditions of Definition 2.2.1 are satisfied. That is for $p \in \mathsf{Prop}$, $u, v \in \mathsf{Tm}$, $c \in \mathsf{Con}$, $A, B \in \mathcal{L}_{\mathsf{PPJ}}$ and $s \in \mathsf{S}$ we have:

(1) $(P_{\geq s}A)^* \in \{\mathsf{T}, \mathsf{F}\}$, $p^* \in \{\mathsf{T}, \mathsf{F}\}$ and $u^* \subseteq \mathcal{L}_{\mathsf{PPJ}}$;

(2) $\left(A \to B \in u^* \text{ and } A \in v^*\right) \implies B \in (u \cdot v)^*$;

(3) $u^* \cup v^* \subseteq (u + v)^*$;

(4) if $(c, A) \in \mathsf{CS}$ then for all $n \in \mathbb{N}$ we have:

$$!^{n-1}c : !^{n-2}c : \cdots : !c : c : A \in (!^n c)^* .$$

Satisfiability under an extended CS-evaluation can be defined in the following way:

Definition 5.3.2 (Satisfiability under an Extended CS-evaluation). Let CS be a constant specification and let $*$ be some extended CS-evaluation. We define what it means for an $\mathcal{L}_{PPJ}$-formula to hold in $*$ as follows:

$$* \models p \iff p^* = \mathsf{T} \quad \text{for } p \in \mathsf{Prop} \ ;$$
$$* \models P_{\geq s}B \iff \left(P_{\geq s}B\right)^* = \mathsf{T} \ ;$$
$$* \models \neg B \iff * \not\models B \ ;$$
$$* \models B \wedge C \iff \left(* \models B \text{ and } * \models C\right) \ ;$$
$$* \models t : B \iff B \in t^* \ .$$

When we say that some $A \in \mathcal{L}_{PPJ}$ is CS-satisfiable, we mean that there exists an extended CS-evaluation that satisfies A.

According to Definition 5.3.1 the satisfiability of an $\mathcal{L}_{PPJ}$ formula under an extended CS-evaluation is similar to the satisfiability of an $\mathcal{L}_J$-formula under a CS-evaluation. Therefore, it makes sense to use an extension of the usual decision procedure for the basic justification logic J (see Section 2.3) to decide whether an $\mathcal{L}_{PPJ}$-formula is CS-satisfiable.

Lemma 5.3.3. *Let CS be a decidable schematic constant specification. For any formula $A \in \mathcal{L}_{PPJ}$, it is decidable whether A is CS-satisfiable.*

Proof. As mentioned earlier we can test whether an $\mathcal{L}_{PPJ}$-formula is CS-satisfiable by extending the decidability algorithm for justification logic J. Most of the algorithm can be easily adapted to our probabilistic setting. The only part of the algorithm that needs major adaptations is the representation of schematic formulas and therefore the unification algorithm.

In the setting of PPJ we need three kinds of schematic variables: for terms, formulas and rational numbers. Because of the side conditions that come with the axioms (WE) and (UN) our schematic formulas should be paired with systems of linear inequalities. For example, the scheme (WE) should be represented by the schematic formula $P_{\leq r}A \rightarrow P_{<s}A$ (with the schematic variables r, s, and A) together with the inequality $r < s$, whereas a scheme that is obtained by a conjunction of the schemata (WE) and (UN) should be represented as

$$\left(P_{\leq r_1}A_1 \rightarrow P_{<s_1}A_1\right) \wedge \left(P_{\leq r_2}A_2 \wedge P_{<s_2}B_2 \rightarrow P_{<r_2+s_2}(A_2 \vee B_2)\right)$$

together with the inequalities

$$\left\{r_1 < s_1, r_2 + s_2 \leq 1\right\} \ .$$

We should not forget that the rational variables belong to S. So we have to add constraints like $0 \leq r \leq 1$.

5.3. DECIDABILITY FOR PPJ

Hence in addition to constructing a substitution, the unification algorithm also has to take care of the linear constraints. For instance, in order to unify the schemata $P_{\geq r}A$ and $P_{\geq s}B$ the algorithm has to unify A and B, and to equate r and s, i.e. it adds $r = s$ to the linear system. In the end, the constructed substitution only is a most general unifier if the linear system is satisfiable. This implies decidability of the $\mathsf{PPJ_{CS,Meas}}$-satisfiability problem since it is well known that satisfiability testing for systems of linear equations is decidable (see e.g. [Lue73]).

Another complication are constraints of the form

$$l = \min(1, r + s) \tag{5.13}$$

that originate from the scheme (DIS). Obviously, Eq. (5.13) is not linear. However, for a linear system C, we find that

$$C \cup \{l = \min(1, r + s)\}$$

has a solution if and only if

$$C \cup \{l = r + s, r + s \leq 1\} \text{ or } C \cup \{l = 1, r + s > 1\}$$

has a solution. Thus we can reduce solving a system involving Eq. (5.13) to solving several linear systems. □

Lemma 5.3.3 is enough for testing whether "justification and classical constraints" can be satisfied. Now we proceed with definitions and lemmata that are needed for testing the satisfiability of "probabilistic constraints".

Definition 5.3.4 (Subformulas and Atoms). The set of subformulas, subf($\cdot$), of an $\mathcal{L}_{\mathsf{PPJ}}$-formula is recursively defined by:

$$\begin{aligned}
\mathsf{subf}(p) &:= \{p\} \quad \text{for } p \in \mathsf{Prop} \ ; \\
\mathsf{subf}(P_{\geq s}A) &:= \{P_{\geq s}A\} \cup \mathsf{subf}(A) \ ; \\
\mathsf{subf}(\neg A) &:= \{\neg A\} \cup \mathsf{subf}(A) \ ; \\
\mathsf{subf}(A \wedge B) &:= \{A \wedge B\} \cup \mathsf{subf}(A) \cup \mathsf{subf}(B) \ ; \\
\mathsf{subf}(t : A) &:= \{t : A\} \cup \mathsf{subf}(A) \ .
\end{aligned}$$

Assume that $\mathsf{subf}(A) = \{A_1, \ldots, A_k\}$ for some $A \in \mathcal{L}_{\mathsf{PPJ}}$. A formula of the form

$$\pm A_1 \wedge \ldots \wedge \pm A_k \ ,$$

where $\pm A_i$ is either A_i or $\neg A_i$, will be called an atom[4] of A. The set $\mathsf{atoms}(A)$ contains all atoms of A.

---
[4] Recall that atoms for $\mathcal{L}_{\mathsf{PJ}}$- and $\mathcal{L}_{\mathsf{PPJ}}$-formulas are defined differently.

Lemma 5.3.5. *Let $M = \langle U, W, H, \mu, * \rangle \in \mathsf{PPJ}_{\mathsf{CS,Meas}}$ and let $A \in \mathcal{L}_{\mathsf{PPJ}}$. Further, let $B \in \mathsf{subf}(A)$, let $C \in \mathsf{atoms}(A)$ and let $w \in U$. Assume that $M, w \models C$. Then we have:*
$$M, w \models B \iff B \in C.$$

Proof. We prove the two directions of the lemma separately:

$\Longleftarrow$: From $B \in C$ and $M, w \models C$ we immediately get $M, w \models B$.

$\Longrightarrow$: Since B is a subformula of A, we have either $B \in C$ or $\neg B \in C$. If $\neg B \in C$, then we would have $M, w \models \neg B$, i.e. $M, w \not\models B$, which contradicts the fact that $M, w \models B$. Thus, we conclude $B \in C$. $\square$

The next lemma is the key for proving decidability of $\mathsf{PPJ}_{\mathsf{CS}}$. It completes the algorithm that we described from the beginning of the section by formally explaining how "justification and classical constraints" and "probabilistic constraints" can be satisfied in the same model. As it will be clear from the proof, the lemma practically states a small model property.

Lemma 5.3.6. *Let CS be a constant specification and let A be an $\mathcal{L}_{\mathsf{PPJ}}$-formula. A is $\mathsf{PPJ}_{\mathsf{CS,Meas}}$-satisfiable if and only if there exists a non-empty set*
$$Y = \{B_1, \ldots, B_n\} \subseteq \mathsf{atoms}(A)$$
such that all of the following conditions hold:

1. *for some $i \in \{1, \ldots, n\}$, $A \in B_i$.*

2. *for every $1 \leq i \leq n$, there exists an extended CS-evaluation that satisfies B_i.*

3. *for every $1 \leq i \leq n$, there are some x_{ij} with $1 \leq j \leq n$, that satisfy the following linear equalities and inequalities:*

$$\sum_{j=1}^{n} x_{ij} = 1$$

$$(\forall 1 \leq j \leq n)\big[x_{ij} \geq 0\big]$$

$$\text{for every } P_{\geq s}C \in B_i, \sum_{\{j | C \in B_j\}} x_{ij} \geq s$$

$$\text{for every } \neg P_{\geq s}C \in B_i, \sum_{\{j | C \in B_j\}} x_{ij} < s \ .$$

5.3. DECIDABILITY FOR PPJ

Proof. Let CS be a constant specification and let $A \in \mathcal{L}_{\mathsf{PPJ}}$. We prove the two directions of the lemma separately:

$\Longrightarrow$: Let $M = \langle U, W, H, \mu, * \rangle \in \mathsf{PPJ}_{\mathsf{CS,Meas}}$. Assume that A is satisfiable in some world of M.

Let $\approx$ denote a binary relation over U such that for all $w, x \in U$ we have:

$$w \approx x \quad \text{if and only if} \quad \big(\forall B \in \mathsf{subf}(A)\big)\big[M, w \models B \Leftrightarrow M, x \models B\big].$$

It is easy to see that $\approx$ is an equivalence relation. Let $K_1, \ldots, K_n$ be the equivalence classes of $\approx$ over U. For every $i \in \{1, \ldots, n\}$ we choose some $w_i \in K_i$. For every $i \in \{1, \ldots, n\}$ some subformulas of A hold in the world w_i and some do not. So, without loss of generality, we assume that for every $i \in \{1, \ldots, n\}$ there exists a $B_i \in \mathsf{atoms}(A)$ such that $M, w_i \models B_i$. For $i \neq j$ we have $B_i \neq B_j$ since w_i and w_j belong to different equivalence classes. Let $Y = \{B_1, \ldots, B_n\}$. Since A holds in some w_i, Y is non-empty. It remains to show that the conditions in the statement of the lemma hold:

1. Let $w \in U$ be such that $M, w \models A$. The world w belongs to some equivalence class of $\approx$ that is represented by w_i. Thus $M, w_i \models A$. By Lemma 5.3.5 we find $A \in B_i$, i.e. condition 1 holds.

2. Let $i \in \{1, \ldots, n\}$. It holds that $M, w_i \models B_i$. We define the extended CS-evaluation $*_i$ as follows (the fact that $*_i$ is an extended CS-evaluation immediately follows from the fact that $*_{w_i}$ is a CS-evaluation):

   - for every $p \in \mathsf{Prop}$:
   $$p^{*_i} = p^*_{w_i} \, ;$$

   - for every $P_{\geq s}B \in \mathcal{L}_{\mathsf{PPJ}}$:
   $$(P_{\geq s}B)^{*_i} = \begin{cases} \mathsf{T} & \text{, if } M, w_i \models P_{\geq s}B \\ \mathsf{F} & \text{, if } M, w_i \not\models P_{\geq s}B \, ; \end{cases}$$

   - for every $t \in \mathsf{Tm}$:
   $$t^{*_i} = t^*_{w_i} \, .$$

   The following statement can be shown by straightforward induction on the complexity of the formula.

   $$\big(\forall B \in \mathsf{subf}(B_i)\big)[M, w_i \models B \Longleftrightarrow *_i \models B] \tag{5.14}$$

   Since, $B_i \in \mathsf{subf}(B_i)$ and $M, w_i \models B_i$, by statement 5.14 we get $*_i \models B_i$. And of course this holds for every $1 \leq i \leq n$. Therefore, condition 2 holds.

3. Let $i \in \{1, \ldots, n\}$. We set

$$y_{ij} = \mu(w_i)(K_j \cap W(w_i)), \text{ for every } 1 \leq j \leq n \ . \tag{5.15}$$

We are going to do some calculations to show that these values y_{ij} satisfy the linear system in condition 3.

First of all we have

$$\sum_{1 \leq j \leq n} y_{ij} =$$
$$\sum_{1 \leq j \leq n} \mu(w_i)(K_j \cap W(w_i)) \stackrel{\text{the } K_j\text{'s are mutually disjoint}}{=}$$
$$\mu(w_i)\Big(\bigcup_{1 \leq j \leq n} \big(K_j \cap W(w_i)\big) \Big) \stackrel{\bigcup_{j=1}^n K_j = U}{=}$$
$$\mu(w_i)\big(W(w_i)\big) \ .$$

And since $\mu(w_i)$ is a finitely additive measure over $W(w_i)$ we get:

$$\sum_{1 \leq j \leq n} y_{ij} = 1 \ . \tag{5.16}$$

By Eq. (5.15) we also have:

$$(\forall 1 \leq j \leq n)\big[y_{ij} \geq 0\big] \ . \tag{5.17}$$

Let $P_{\geq s}C \in B_i$. Since $M, w_i \models B_i$ it also holds that $M, w_i \models P_{\geq s}C$, i.e.

$$\mu(w_i)([C]_{M,w_i}) \geq s \ . \tag{5.18}$$

We will prove that:

$$\bigcup_{\{j | C \in B_j\}} \big(K_j \cap W(w_i)\big) = [C]_{M,w_i} \ . \tag{5.19}$$

Let $w \in [C]_{M,w_i}$. We have $w \in W(w_i)$ and $M, w \models C$. w must belong to some K_j. We also have that $M, w_j \models C$ and $M, w_j \models B_j$, which by Lemma 5.3.5 implies $C \in B_j$. Thus, we proved that there exists some j such that $C \in B_j$ and $w \in K_j \cap W(w_i)$. Thus

$$w \in \bigcup_{\{j | C \in B_j\}} \big(K_j \cap W(w_i)\big) \ .$$

5.3. DECIDABILITY FOR PPJ

On the other hand let $w \in \bigcup_{\{j|C \in B_j\}} \left(K_j \cap W(w_i)\right)$. So, there exists some j, such that $C \in B_j$ and $w \in K_j \cap W(w_i)$. It holds that $M, w_j \models B_j$ and since $w \in K_j$ we have that $M, w \models B_j$ which implies that $M, w \models C$. So, since $w \in W(w_i)$, we have that $w \in [C]_{M,w_i}$.

Therefore Eq. (5.19) holds.

By Eq. (5.18) and Eq. (5.19) we get:

$$\mu(w_i)\left(\bigcup_{\{j|C \in B_j\}} \left(K_j \cap W(w_i)\right)\right) \geq s \ .$$

Since the K_j's are mutually disjoint and $\mu(w_i)$ is a finitely additive measure we have:

$$\sum_{\{j|C \in B_j\}} \mu(w_i)\left(K_j \cap W(w_i)\right) \geq s$$

and by Eq. (5.15):

$$\sum_{\{j|C \in B_j\}} y_{ij} \geq s \ .$$

So we proved that

$$\text{for every } P_{\geq s}C \in B_i, \sum_{\{j|C \in B_j\}} y_{ij} \geq s \ . \tag{5.20}$$

By a similar reasoning we can prove that

$$\text{for every } \neg P_{\geq s}C \in B_i, \sum_{\{j|C \in B_j\}} y_{ij} < s \ . \tag{5.21}$$

By Eqs. (5.16), (5.17), (5.20) and (5.21) we have that the y_{ij}'s satisfy the linear system in condition 3.

$\Longleftarrow$: Assume that there exists some $Y = \{B_1, \ldots, B_n\} \subseteq \text{atoms}(A)$ such that conditions 1–3 in the lemma's statement hold. For every $1 \leq i \leq n$, let $*_i$ be an extended CS-evaluation such that $*_i \models B_i$ (by condition 2 we know that such an extended CS-evaluation exists). Let x_{ij}, for $i, j \in \{1, \ldots, n\}$, be numbers that satisfy the linear system in condition 3.

We define the quintuple $M = \langle U, W, H, \mu, * \rangle$ as follows:

- $U = \{w_1, \ldots, w_n\}$ for some $w_1, \ldots, w_n$.

- For all $1 \leq i \leq n$ we set:

    1. $W(w_i) = U$;
    2. $H(w_i) = \mathcal{P}(W(w_i))$;
    3. for every $V \in H(w_i)$:
    $$\mu(w_i)(V) = \sum_{\{j \mid w_j \in V\}} x_{ij} \; ;$$
    4. for every $p \in \mathsf{Prop}$:
    $$p^*_{w_i} = p^*_i$$
    and for every $t \in \mathsf{Tm}$:
    $$t^*_{w_i} = t^*_i \; .$$

First we show that $M \in \mathsf{PPJ}_{\mathsf{CS},\mathsf{Meas}}$. Since Y is non-empty, n is positive thus U is non-empty too. Let $1 \leq i \leq n$. It holds that:

(i) $H(w_i)$ is an algebra over $W(w_i)$, since $H(w_i)$ is the powerset of $W(w_i)$.

(ii) For every $A \in \mathcal{L}_{\mathsf{PPJ}}$ we have that $[A]_{M,w_i} \in \mathcal{P}(W(w_i))$, i.e. $[A]_{M,w_i} \in H(w_i)$.

(iii) $\mu(w_i)$ is defined for all $V \in H(w_i)$ and by the first two lines of the linear system in condition 3 it holds that the codomain of $\mu(w_i)$ is $[0,1]$.

We also have that:
$$\mu(w_i)(W(w_i)) = \mu(w_i)(U) = \sum_{\{j \mid w_j \in U\}} x_{ij} = \sum_{1 \leq j \leq n} x_{ij} = 1 \; .$$

Let $U, V \in H(w_i)$ such that $U \cap V = \emptyset$. It holds
$$\mu(w_i)(U \cup V) = \sum_{\{j \mid w_j \in U \cup V\}} x_{ij}$$
$$= \sum_{\{j \mid w_j \in U\}} x_{ij} + \sum_{\{j \mid w_j \in V\}} x_{ij}$$
$$= \mu(w_i)(U) + \mu(w_i)(V) \; .$$

Thus, $\mu(w_i)$ is a finitely additive measure over $H(w_i)$.

(iv) The fact that $*_i$ is an extended CS-evaluation immediately implies that $*_{w_i}$ is a CS-evaluation.

5.3. DECIDABILITY FOR PPJ

From **(i)** - **(iv)** we conclude that $M \in \mathsf{PPJ}_{\mathsf{CS},\mathsf{Meas}}$. It remains to show $M, w_i \models A$ for some i.

First we have to show the following statement:

$$(\forall D \in \mathsf{subf}(A))(\forall 1 \leq i \leq n)\Big[D \in B_i \iff M, w_i \models D\Big]. \qquad (5.22)$$

Let $D \in B_i$. We will prove statement (5.22) by induction on the structure of D. Let $1 \leq i \leq n$. We distinguish the following cases:

$D \equiv p \in \mathsf{Prop}$: It holds:

$$\begin{aligned}
D \in B_i &\iff \\
p \in B_i &\iff \\
*_i \models p &\iff \\
p^{*_i} = \mathsf{T} &\iff \\
p^*_{w_i} = \mathsf{T} &\iff \\
M, w_i \models p &\iff \\
M, w_i \models D\,.
\end{aligned}$$

$D \equiv t : C$: We have:

$$\begin{aligned}
D \in B_i &\iff \\
t : C \in B_i &\iff \\
*_i \models t : C &\iff \\
C \in t^{*_i} &\iff \\
C \in t^*_{w_i} &\iff \\
M, w_i \models t : C &\iff \\
M, w_i \models D\,.
\end{aligned}$$

$D \equiv P_{\geq s} C$. We prove the two directions of the claim separately.

$\Longrightarrow$: Assume that $D \in B_i$, i.e. $P_{\geq s} C \in B_i$. By the third line of the linear system in condition 3 we have:

$$\sum_{\{j \mid C \in B_j\}} x_{ij} \geq s\,.$$

By the inductive hypothesis we have:

$$\sum_{\{j \mid M, w_j \models C\}} x_{ij} \geq s\,. \qquad (5.23)$$

It holds that
$$[C]_{M,w_i} = \{w_j \in W(w_i) \mid M, w_j \models C\} = \{w_j \mid M, w_j \models C\} . \quad (5.24)$$
By the definition of M we have:
$$\mu(w_i)([C]_{M,w_i}) = \sum_{\{j \mid w_j \in [C]_{M,w_i}\}} x_{ij} \stackrel{(5.24)}{=} \sum_{\{j \mid M, w_j \models C\}} x_{ij} .$$
And by (5.23) we have that
$$\mu(w_i)([C]_{M,w_i}) \geq s$$
i.e.
$$M, w_i \models P_{\geq s} C$$
i.e.
$$M, w_i \models D .$$
$\Longleftarrow$: Let $M, w_i \models D$. Assume that $D \notin B_i$, i.e. $\neg D \in B_i$, that is:
$$\neg P_{\geq s} C \in B_i .$$
By the last line of the linear system in condition 3 we have that
$$\sum_{j : C \in B_j} x_{ij} < s .$$
By using a similar argument as before we can prove that
$$\mu(w_i)([C]_{M,w_i}) < s$$
i.e.
$$M, w_i \not\models D$$
which is absurd. Therefore $D \in B_i$.

$D \equiv D_1 \wedge D_2$: Here $D \in B_i$ means
$$D_1 \wedge D_2 \in B_i . \quad (5.25)$$
We know that $*_i \models B_i$. Assume that $D_1 \notin B_i$ or $D_2 \notin B_i$. Then it should be $\neg D_1 \in B_i$ or $\neg D_2 \in B_i$, i.e. $*_i \not\models D_1$ or $*_i \not\models D_2$. But this is absurd since we have that $*_i \models D_1 \wedge D_2$. So, both D_1 and D_2 belong to B_i. Hence (5.25) is equivalent to the following statements.

$$\begin{aligned} D_1 \in B_i \text{ and } D_2 \in B_i & \quad \stackrel{\text{i.h.}}{\Longleftrightarrow} \\ M, w_i \models D_1 \text{ and } M, w_i \models D_2 & \quad \Longleftrightarrow \\ M, w_i \models D_1 \wedge D_2 & \quad \Longleftrightarrow \\ M, w_i \models D . \end{aligned}$$

5.3. DECIDABILITY FOR PPJ

$D \equiv \neg D'$: We have:

$$D \in B_i \iff$$
$$\neg D' \in B_i \iff$$
$$D' \notin B_i \stackrel{\text{i.h.}}{\iff}$$
$$M, w_i \not\models D' \iff$$
$$M, w_i \models \neg D' \iff$$
$$M, w_i \models D \ .$$

We conclude that statement (5.22) holds.

We have $A \in \mathsf{subf}(A)$. Thus, by statement (5.22) we find:

$$(\forall 1 \leq i \leq n)\Big[A \in B_i \iff M, w_i \models A\Big] \ .$$

By condition 1, there exists an i such that $A \in B_i$. Thus, there exists an i such that $M, w_i \models A$. Hence, A is $\mathsf{PPJ}_{\mathsf{CS},\mathsf{Meas}}$-satisfiable. □

In the proof of Lemma 5.3.6 we construct a model with at most $2^{|\mathsf{subf}(A)|}$ worlds that satisfies A. Hence a corollary of Lemma 5.3.6 is that any $A \in \mathcal{L}_{\mathsf{PPJ}}$ is $\mathsf{PPJ}_{\mathsf{CS},\mathsf{Meas}}$-satisfiable if and only if it is satisfiable in a $\mathsf{PPJ}_{\mathsf{CS},\mathsf{Meas}}$-model with at most $2^{|\mathsf{subf}(A)|}$ worlds. In other words, Lemma 5.3.6 implies a small model property for $\mathsf{PPJ}_{\mathsf{CS}}$. Moreover, Lemma 5.3.6 dictates a procedure to decide the satisfiability problem for $\mathsf{PPJ}_{\mathsf{CS}}$.

Theorem 5.3.7. *Let* CS *be a decidable and schematic constant specification. The* $\mathsf{PPJ}_{\mathsf{CS},\mathsf{Meas}}$-*satisfiability problem is decidable.*

Proof. Let CS be a decidable almost schematic constant specification and let $A \in \mathcal{L}_{\mathsf{PPJ}}$. The formula A is satisfiable if and only if for some $Y \subseteq \mathsf{atoms}(A)$ all conditions in the statement of Lemma 5.3.6 hold. Since $\mathsf{atoms}(A)$ is finite, it suffices to show that for every $Y \subseteq \mathsf{atoms}(A)$ the conditions 1–3 in the statement of Lemma 5.3.6 can be effectively checked:

- Decidability of condition 1 is trivial.
- Decidability of condition 2 follows from Lemma 5.3.3.
- In condition 3 we have to check for the satisfiability of a set of linear inequalities. There are several decision procedures available for this problem (see, for example, [Lue73]).

We conclude that the $\mathsf{PPJ}_{\mathsf{CS},\mathsf{Meas}}$-satisfiability problem is decidable. □

Chapter 6

Conclusion and Further Work

This thesis provides a first extensive study of uncertain reasoning in justification logic. We investigated how probabilistic logic and justification logic can be combined in order to obtain probabilistic justification logics that allow the analysis of epistemic situations with incomplete information. The language of our logics is defined by adding probability operators to the language of justification logic. Syntax of our logics consists of the usual axioms for probability combined with the axioms for justification logic. In order to give semantics to our logics we combined the standard model for probability with ontological models for justification logics in what turned out to be a Kripke-style semantics for our logics. Note that we had to rely on an infinitary rule in order to obtain strong completeness. We proved decidability results for our logics and in the case where no iterations of the probability operators are allowed we proved that the computational complexity of the probabilistic justification logic remains the same as the complexity of the underlying justification logic.

The main directions for further research can be divided in two categories:

A. Extending the logical framework for probabilistic reasoning in justification logics.

As the reader has noticed, in this thesis we only studied the enrichment of the basic justification logic J with probabily operators. The main reason for this restriction is that in the first study of the probabilistic extension of justification logic we wanted to focus on the simplest possible framework. However the probabilistic extension of more complicated justification logics than J is also worth studying.

For example the factivity axiom

$$t : A \to A$$

or the positive introspection axiom

$$t : A \to !t : t : A$$

can be added to the logic PPJ, so that we can have a probabilistic version of the famous Logic of Proofs (LP).

Another idea for extending the logics presented in this thesis is to study multi-agent systems. Consider again the Motivating Example from Chapter 1. In the example there are three agents:

agent i: Peter

agent j: Marc

agent k: the New York Times

Assume also that t stands for "Marc said so" and A stands for "the tax rates will increase".

So far we considered only single-agent probabilistic justification logics. However, we can describe the situation in the Motivating Example more precisely, using formulas of the form: $P_{i,\geq s}(t :_j A)$ meaning that agent i puts probability at least s to the fact that agent j considers t as evidence for statement A. Naturally this requires building a multi-agent probabilistic justification logic, where each agent is able to use their own machinery for constructing evidence and determining probabilities. It is also interesting to allow the agents the ability to interact and to use different kind of reasoning methods, that is to let them use different logical systems.

A further extension would be to investigate some cases where statistical evidence can serve as justifications. For instance, if we know that the conditional probability of B given A is s, it seems natural to use A (or, better, a justification term $h(A)$ that is obtained from the formula A) as a justification for B with probability s. Thus, it would be interesting to study a system that has an axiom like the following:

$$P_{\geq s}(B|A) \to P_{\geq s}(h(A) : B) .$$

B. Studying the computational complexity of (probabilistic) justification logics

Although we have decision procedures for the logic PPJ, we have not established complexity bounds for this logic yet. We already know that one iteration of the probability operator does not increase the computational complexity of the logic, since the complexity of **PJ** remains the same as the complexity of the underlying logic **J**. However, it has been proved in the literature that arbitrary iterations of the probability operator lead to combinatorial explosion in the complexity of the logic. For example, the satisfiability problem for the logic **LPP**$_1$ [ORM09], which is a probabilistic logic with the same design as that of **PPJ**, is in **PSPACE**. Furthermore in [FH94] it is proved that the satisfiability problem of a logic similar to **PPJ**, that allows iterations of knowledge and probability operators, is **PSPACE**-complete. For the above reasons we conjecture that satisfiability testing for the logic **PPJ** should also be **PSPACE**-complete.

Traditional computational complexity theory attempts to characterize the complexity of a problem as a function of the input size n. Parameterized complexity theory [DF99, FG06] requires for every problem the definition of a structural parameter k, which attempts to capture the aspect of the problem which causes its intractability. One of the central notions in this theory is called fixed-parameter tractability (FPT): an algorithm is called FPT if it runs in time $\mathcal{O}(f(k) \cdot n^c)$, where f is any computable function and c a constant. The design of FPT-algorithms for justification logics and probabilistic justification logics can lead to better understanding of the reasons that cause the combinatorial explosion of the satisfiability problem in these logics.

Bibliography

[Ach15] Antonis Achilleos. Nexp-completeness and universal hardness results for justification logic. CSR 2015: 27-52, 2015. 16

[AF15]   Sergei Artemov and Melvin Fitting. Justification logic. In Edward N. Zalta, editor, *The Stanford Encyclopedia of Philosophy*. Winter 2015 edition, 2015. 1, 5, 13

[Art95] Sergei N. Artemov. Operational modal logic. Technical Report MSI 95–29, Cornell University, December 1995. 1, 15

[Art01] Sergei N. Artemov. Explicit provability and constructive semantics. *Bulletin of Symbolic Logic*, 7(1):1–36, March 2001. 1, 2, 14

[Art12] Sergei N. Artemov. The ontology of justifications in the logical setting. *Studia Logica*, 100(1–2):17–30, April 2012. Published online February 2012. 2, 14, 54

[Art16] Sergei N. Artëmov. On aggregating probabilistic evidence. In Sergei N. Artëmov and Anil Nerode, editors, *Logical Foundations of Computer Science - International Symposium, LFCS 2016, Deerfield Beach, FL, USA, January 4-7, 2016. Proceedings*, volume 9537 of *Lecture Notes in Computer Science*, pages 27–42. Springer, 2016. 6

[BdRV01] Patrick Blackburn, Maarten de Rijke, and Yde Venema. *Modal Logic*. Cambridge University Press, New York, NY, USA, 2001. 1

[BK12]   Samuel R. Buss and Roman Kuznets. Lower complexity bounds in justification logic. *Annals of Pure and Applied Logic*, 163(7):888–905, July 2012. 16

[BKS11a] Samuel Bucheli, Roman Kuznets, and Thomas Studer. Justifications for common knowledge. *Journal of Applied Non-Classical Logics*, 21(1):35–60, January–March 2011. 2

[BKS11b] Samuel Bucheli, Roman Kuznets, and Thomas Studer. Partial realization in dynamic justification logic. In Lev D. Beklemishev and Ruy de Queiroz, editors, *Logic, Language, Information and Computation, 18th International Workshop, WoLLIC 2011, Philadelphia, PA, USA, May 18–20, 2011, Proceedings*, volume 6642 of *Lecture Notes in Artificial Intelligence*, pages 35–51. Springer, 2011. 2

[BKS14] Samuel Bucheli, Roman Kuznets, and Thomas Studer. Realizing public announcements by justifications. *J. Comput. Syst. Sci.*, 80(6):1046–1066, 2014. 2

[Bre00] Vladimir N. Brezhnev. On explicit counterparts of modal logics. Technical Report CFIS 2000–05, Cornell University, 2000. 2

[Chv83] Vašek Chvátal. *Linear programming*. W. H. Freeman and Company, New York, 1983. 65

[DF99] Rodney G. Downey and Michael R. Fellows. *Parameterized Complexity*. Monographs in Computer Science. Springer, 1999. 91

[FG06] Jörg Flum and Martin Grohe. *Parameterized Complexity Theory*. Texts in Theoretical Computer Science. An EATCS Series. Springer, 2006. 91

[FH94] Ronald Fagin and Joseph Y. Halpern. Reasoning about knowledge and probability. *J. ACM*, 41(2):340–367, 1994. 91

[FHM90] Ronald Fagin, Joseph Y. Halpern, and Nimrod Megiddo. A logic for reasoning about probabilities. *Inf. Comput.*, 87(1/2):78–128, 1990. 3, 63, 67

[Fit05] Melvin Fitting. The logic of proofs, semantically. *Annals of Pure and Applied Logic*, 132(1):1–25, February 2005. 2

[FL15] Tuan-Fang Fan and Churn-Jung Liau. A logic for reasoning about justified uncertain beliefs. In Qiang Yang and Michael Wooldridge, editors, *Proc. IJCAI 2015*, pages 2948–2954. AAAI Press, 2015. 5

[Fol09] Richard Foley. Beliefs, Degrees of Belief, and the Lockean Thesis. In F. Huber and C. Schmidt-Petri, editors, *Degrees of Belief*, pages 37–47. Springer, 2009. 34

[Gha14] M. Ghari. Justification logics in a fuzzy setting. *ArXiv e-prints*, July 2014. 5

BIBLIOGRAPHY 95

[Kei77]   Jerome Keisler. Hyperfinite model theory. In R. O. Gandy and J. M. E. Hyland, editors, *Logic Colloquim 1976*, LNCS, page 5–10. North-Holland, 1977. 2

[KMOS15] Ioannis Kokkinis, Petar Maksimović, Zoran Ognjanović, and Thomas Studer. First steps towards probabilistic justification logic. *Logic Journal of the IGPL*, 23(4):662–687, 2015. 4, 7, 17

[Kok16]   Ioannis Kokkinis. The complexity of non-iterated probabilistic justification logic. In Marc Gyssens and Guillermo Ricardo Simari, editors, *Foundations of Information and Knowledge Systems - 9th International Symposium, FoIKS 2016, Linz, Austria, March 7-11, 2016. Proceedings*, volume 9616 of *Lecture Notes in Computer Science*, pages 292–310. Springer, 2016. 7, 63

[KOS16]   Ioannis Kokkinis, Zoran Ognjanović, and Thomas Studer. Probabilistic justification logic. In Sergei N. Artëmov and Anil Nerode, editors, *Logical Foundations of Computer Science - International Symposium, LFCS 2016, Deerfield Beach, FL, USA, January 4-7, 2016. Proceedings*, volume 9537 of *Lecture Notes in Computer Science*, pages 174–186. Springer, 2016. 5, 7, 17, 30, 63

[KS12]   Roman Kuznets and Thomas Studer. Justifications, ontology, and conservativity. In Thomas Bolander, Torben Braüner, Silvio Ghilardi, and Lawrence Moss, editors, *Advances in Modal Logic, Volume 9*, pages 437–458. College Publications, 2012. 2, 14, 54

[KS13]   Roman Kuznets and Thomas Studer. Update as evidence: Belief expansion. In Sergei [N.] Artemov and Anil Nerode, editors, *Logical Foundations of Computer Science, International Symposium, LFCS 2013, San Diego, CA, USA, January 6-8, 2013, Proceedings*, volume 7734 of *Lecture Notes in Computer Science*, pages 266–279. Springer, 2013. 2

[KSar]   Roman Kuznets and Thomas Studer. Weak arithmetical interpretations for the logic of proofs. *Logic Journal of IGPL*, to appear. 1

[Kuz00]   Roman Kuznets. On the complexity of explicit modal logics. In Peter G. Clote and Helmut Schwichtenberg, editors, *Computer Science Logic, 14th International Workshop, CSL 2000, Annual Conference of the EACSL, Fischbachau, Germany, August 21–26, 2000, Proceedings*, volume 1862 of *Lecture Notes in Computer Science*, pages 371–383. Springer, 2000. Errata concerning the explicit counterparts of $\mathcal{D}$ and $\mathcal{D}4$ are published as [Kuz09]. 12, 15, 63, 74

[Kuz08]   Roman Kuznets. *Complexity Issues in Justification Logic*. PhD thesis, City University of New York, May 2008. 15, 63

[Kuz09]   Roman Kuznets. Complexity through tableaux in justification logic. In *2008 European Summer Meeting of the Association for Symbolic Logic, Logic Colloquium '08, Bern, Switzerland, July 3–July 8, 2008*, volume 15(1) of *Bulletin of Symbolic Logic*, page 121. Association for Symbolic Logic, March 2009. Abstract. 95

[Kyb61]   Henry E. Jr. Kyburg. *Probability and the Logic of Rational Belief*. Wesleyan University Press, 1961. 5, 17, 34

[Lei14]   Hannes Leitgeb. The stability theory of belief. *Philosophical Review*, 123(2):131–171, 2014. 35

[Lue73]   David G. Luenberger. *Introduction to Linear and Nonlinear Programming*. Addison-Wesley, 1973. 79, 87

[Mil07]   Robert [S.] Milnikel. Derivability in certain subsystems of the Logic of Proofs is Π_2^p-complete. *Annals of Pure and Applied Logic*, 145(3):223–239, March 2007. 16

[Mil14]   Robert S. Milnikel. The logic of uncertain justifications. *Annals of Pure and Applied Logic*, 165(1):305–315, January 2014. Published online in August 2013. 5

[Mkr97]   Alexey Mkrtychev. Models for the logic of proofs. In Sergei Adian and Anil Nerode, editors, *Logical Foundations of Computer Science, 4th International Symposium, LFCS'97, Yaroslavl, Russia, July 6–12, 1997, Proceedings*, volume 1234 of *Lecture Notes in Computer Science*, pages 266–275. Springer, 1997. 2, 12, 15

[Nil86]   Nils J. Nilsson. Probabilistic logic. *Artif. Intell.*, 28(1):71–87, 1986. 2

[OR99]   Zoran Ognjanović and Miodrag Rašković. Some probability logics with new types of probability operators. *Journal of Logic and Computation*, 9(2):181–195, 1999. 3

[OR00]   Zoran Ognjanović and Miodrag Rašković. Some first order probability. *Theoretical Computer Science*, 247:191–212, 2000. 3

[ORM09]   Zoran Ognjanović, Miodrag Rašković, and Zoran Marković. Probability logics. *Zbornik radova, subseries "Logic in Computer Science"*, 12(20):35–111, 2009. 2, 4, 5, 54, 63, 67, 91

[Pap94]   Christos H. Papadimitriou. *Computational complexity*. Addison-Wesley, 1994. 15

[RO99]   Miodrag Rašković and Zoran Ognjanović. A first order probability logic, $LP_\mathbb{Q}$. *Publications de L'Institute Matematique (Belgrad)*, ns. 65 (79):1–7, 1999. 3

[Sch15]   L. Menasché Schechter. A logic of plausible justifications. *Theor. Comput. Sci.*, 603:132–145, 2015. 6

[SO14]   Angelina Ilić Stepić and Zoran Ognjanović. Complex valued probability logics. *Publications de l'Institut Mathématique (N.S.)*, 95(109):73–86, 2014. 3

[Stu12]   Thomas Studer. Lectures on justification logic. Lecture notes, November 2012. 1

Index

□, 2
CS-evaluation, 12
$\mathsf{J_{CS}}$, 11
$\mathbb{N}$, 37
$\mathsf{PJ_{CS}}$, 19
$\mathsf{PPJ_{CS}}$, 30
Prop, 10
atoms(·), 79
$\log_2(\cdot)$, 65
$\models$, 13, 22, 32
sup, 43, 55

algebra, 20, 56
algorithm, 15, 66
  completion, 15, 74
  saturation, 15, 74
  unification, 78
application axiom, 25
Artemov, Sergei, 1, 15
atom, 64, 79
atomic proposition, 10
axiom instance, 11
axiom scheme, 11, 18, 31

Bernoulli, Jacobus, 2
Boole, George, 2

cardinal number, 64
codomain, 49, 57, 84
coefficient, 65
complexity bounds
  lower, 63, 75
  upper, 63
complexity class

coNP, 74
P, 73
NP, 75
Π_2^p-complete, 16, 76
Σ_2^p, 16, 74
Σ_2^p-complete, 16, 76
Σ_2^p-hard, 16, 75
$\mathsf{NP^{NP}}$, 75
NP-complete, 3
computational complexity, 15
consistent sets, 42
constant specification, 11, 20
  axiomatically appropriate, 11,
    14, 16, 28, 75
  decidable, 11, 15, 16, 74
  finite, 11, 15
  schematic, 11, 15, 74, 87
  total, 11
Cramer's rule, 67

decision problem, 14, 23, 33, 34
deductive system, 11, 19, 30
deductively closed, 12
denominator, 67
derivability problem
  in $\mathsf{J_{CS}}$, 14
  in $\mathsf{PJ_{CS}}$, 23
  in $\mathsf{PPJ_{CS}}$, 34
determinant, 66
domain, 32, 49, 57

enumeration, 45
equivalence class, 81
equivalence relation, 81

extended CS-evaluation, 77

Fagin, Ronald, 3
Fan, Tuan-Fang, 6
finitely additive measure, 20, 50
Fitting, Melvin, 2
Foley, Richard, 34

Ghari, Meghdad, 6
grammar, 9, 10, 17, 30

Halpern, Joseph Y., 3
Henkin, Leon, 37, 41
Hilbert, David, 30

independence, 29
independent sets, 21
infinitary rule, 3, 42
internalization, 14
    probabilistic, 28
intuitionistic logic, 1
iterations, 30

justification assertion, 9, 64
justification logic, 1
    J, 2
    LP, 2, 15, 90

Keisler, H. Jerome, 2
Kripke, Saul, 2
Kuznets, Roman, 2, 12, 74
Kyburg, Henry E. Jr., 5, 34

language, 10, 17, 30
Leibnitz, Gottfried Wilhelm, 2
Leitgeb, Hannes, 35
lemma
    Lindenbaum, 45
    truth for PJ, 53
    truth for PPJ, 60
Liau, Churn-Jung, 6
linear equation, 79
linear inequality, 78

linear programming, 63
linear system, 79
linearly dependent, 66
Lockean thesis, 34
lottery paradox, 34

maximal consistent set, 54
measurable set, 20
Meggido, Nimrod, 3
Milnikel, Bob, 6
Mkrtychev, Alexey, 2, 12, 15
modal logic, 1, 2, 14, 25
    K, 2
    S4, 2
model, 20
    PJ_{CS}-model, 20
    PPJ_{CS}-model, 31
    basic modular, 2
    canonical for PJ, 48
    canonical for PPJ, 54
    Kripke, 2, 3
    measurable, 21, 32
most general unifier, 16

necessitation
    constructive, 14, 29
    probabilistic, 29
    rule, 14
Nilsson, Nils, 2
numerator, 67

operators' precedence, 9
oracle, 75

Plato, 1
polynomial time, 11, 74
possible world, 31
powerset, 12
probability space, 20, 31, 54, 56
property
    Archimedean, 37
    small model, 67, 87

INDEX

quintuple, 54

rational belief, 34
rational number, 6, 52, 64, 67
real number, 37, 39
relatively prime, 64
rule of inference, 19

satisfiability problem
    $PJ_{CS,Meas}$-satisfiability, 23
    $PPJ_{CS,Meas}$-satisfiability, 33
    in J_{CS}, 14
schematic formulas, 78
schematic variables, 78
semantical characterization, 29
semantical consequence, 13, 23, 33
    global, 33
    local, 33
size function, 64
stability theory of belief, 35
stable set, 35
structure, 20
Studer, Thomas, 2
subformula, 79
substitution, 79
supremum, 43, 49, 55
syntactical characterization, 29

theorem
    compactness, 3, 42
    completeness, 15
    deduction, 14, 24
    internalization, 14
    probabilistic internalization, 28
    simple completeness, 3
    soundness, 15, 40
    strong completeness, 3
    strong completeness for PJ, 41
    strong completeness for PPJ, 62
transfinite induction, 37, 40
truth value, 12, 58

undecidable, 15
upper bound, 74

vector, 65

Erklärung
gemäss Art. 28 Abs. 2 RSL 05

Name/Vorname: Kokkinis Ioannis

Matrikelnummer: 12-129-771

Studiengang: Informatik

Bachelor ☐ Master ☐ Dissertation ☒

Titel der Arbeit: Uncertain Reasoning in Justification Logic

LeiterIn der Arbeit: Prof. Dr. Thomas Studer

Ich erkläre hiermit, dass ich diese Arbeit selbständig verfasst und keine anderen als die angegebenen Quellen benutzt habe. Alle Stellen, die wörtlich oder sinngemäss aus Quellen entnommen wurden, habe ich als solche gekennzeichnet. Mir ist bekannt, dass andernfalls der Senat gemäss Artikel 36 Absatz 1 Buchstabe r des Gesetzes vom 5. September 1996 über die Universität zum Entzug des auf Grund dieser Arbeit verliehenen Titels berechtigt ist. Ich gewähre hiermit Einsicht in diese Arbeit.

Bern, den 20. Juni 2016

....
Unterschrift

Lebenslauf

1986	*Geboren*
	am 26. Mai in Athen, Griechenland
1992-2004	*Grundschule und Gymnasium*
	an der Arsakeio-Schule in Psychiko, Athen
2004-2010	*Diplom in Electrical und Computer Engineering*
	an der Nationalen Technischen Universität von Athen
2010-2011	*Militärdienst*
	in Alexandroupolis, Griechenland
2011-2015	*Master in Theoretischer Informatik*
	an der Nationalen und Kapodistrianen Universität von Athen
2012-2016	*Doktorand (Studiengang Informatik)*
	bei Prof. Dr. Thomas Studer an der Universität Bern, Forschungsgruppe "Logic and Theory Group"